marc
chagall
my life

TRANSLATED BY ELISABETH ABBOTT

WITH TWENTY ILLUSTRATIONS

BY THE AUTHOR

This first publication in English of Marc Chagall's early autobiography is of importance to all those interested in the formation and development of one of the most popular artists of this century. In addition, *My Life* presents a warm, delightful picture of village life in Russia at the turn of the century as well as a sensitive view of the artist's life in Paris in the years immediately preceding World War I.

Chagall the author has the same poetic richness and happy fantasy with which Chagall the artist entrances us. His autobiography, which he finished in 1922, describes with the same primitive joy the world of imagination of Marc C
work.

*Translated from the French
by Elisabeth Abbott*

marc chagall my life

The Orion Press

New York

First printing
All rights reserved
© *1960 by Marc Chagall*
Illustrations printed by IMAGO, Zurich, Switzerland
Text printed and volume bound by
The Haddon Craftsmen, Inc., Scranton, Pa.
Designed by Wladislaw Finne

Library of Congress Catalog Card Number: 60-8361

illustrations

marc chagall my life

1

The first thing I ever saw was a trough. Simple, square, half hollow, half oval. A market trough. Once inside, I filled it completely.

I don't remember—perhaps my mother told me—but at the very moment I was born a great fire broke out, in a little cottage, behind a prison, near the highroad, on the outskirts of Vitebsk.

The town was on fire, the quarter where the poor Jews lived.

They carried the bed and the mattress, the mother and the babe at her feet, to a safe place at the other end of town.

But, first of all, I was born dead.

I did not want to live. Imagine a white bubble that does not want to live. As if it had been stuffed with Chagall pictures.

They pricked that bubble with needles, they plunged it into a pail of water. At last it emitted a feeble whimper.

But the main thing was, I was born dead.

I hope the psychologists have the grace not to draw improper conclusions from that!

However, that little house near the Pestkowatik road had not been touched. I saw it not so long ago.

As soon as he was a little better off, my father sold the cottage. The place reminds me of the bump on the head of the rabbi in green I painted, or of a potato tossed into a barrel of herring and soaked in pickling brine. Looking at this cottage from the height of my recent "grandeur," I winced and I asked myself:

"How could I possibly have been born here? How does one breathe?"

However, when my grandfather, with the long, black beard, died in all honor, my father, for a few roubles, bought another place.

In that neighborhood, no longer near an insane asylum as at Pestkowatik. All about us, churches, fences, shops, synagogues—simple and eternal, like the buildings in the frescoes of Giotto.

Around me come and go, turn and turn, or just trot along, all sorts of Jews, old and young, Javitches and Bejlines. A beggar runs towards his house, a rich man goes home. The cheder boy runs home. Papa goes home.

In those days there was no cinema.

People went home or to the shop. That is what I remember after my trough.

I say nothing of the sky, of the stars of my childhood.

They are my stars, my sweet stars; they accompany me to school and wait for me on the street till I return. Poor dears, forgive me. I have left you alone on such a dizzy height!

My town, sad and gay!

As a boy, I used to watch you from our doorstep, childishly. To a child's eyes you were clear. When the walls cut off my view, I climbed up on a little post. If then I still could not see you, I climbed up on the roof. Why not? My grandfather used to climb up there too.

And I gazed at you as much as I pleased.

Here, in Pokrowskaja Street, I was born a second time.

Have you sometimes seen, in Florentine paintings, one of those men whose beard is never trimmed, with eyes at once brown and ash-gray, with the complexion the color of burnt-ochre and all lines and wrinkles?

That is my father.

Or perhaps you have seen one of the figures in the Haggadah, with their sheeplike expressions (Forgive me, dear father!).

You remember I made a study of you. Your portrait was to have had the effect of a candle that bursts into flame and goes out at the same moment. Its aroma—that of sleep.

A fly buzzing around—curse it!—and because of it I fall asleep.

Must I talk about my father?

What is a man worth if he is worth nothing? If he is priceless? That is why it is difficult for me to find the right words for him.

My grandfather, a teacher of religion, could think of nothing better than to place my father—his first-born son —still in childhood, as a clerk in a herring plant, and his youngest son with a hairdresser.

No, my father was not a clerk but, for thirty-two years, simply a laborer.

He lifted heavy barrels and my heart used to twist like a Turkish bagel as I watched him lift those weights and stir the herring with his frozen hands. His huge boss would stand to one side like a stuffed animal.

My father's clothes sometimes shone with herring brine. Farther off, light from above would fall into reflections on every side. Alone, his face, now yellow, now white, would faintly smile from time to time.

What a smile! Where did it come from?

4   It whispered of the street where dim passers-by roamed about, reflecting the moonlight. Suddenly, I saw his teeth shine. They made me think of a cat's teeth, of a cow's teeth, of any teeth.

Everything about my father seemed to me enigma and sadness. An image inaccessible.

Always tired, always pensive, his eyes alone gave forth a soft reflection of a grayish-blue.

In his greasy, work-soiled clothes, a handkerchief of dull red showing at one of the big pockets, he would come home, tall and thin. The evening came in with him.

From his pocket he would draw a pile of cakes, of frozen pears. With his brown and wrinkled hand he'd pass them out to us children. They were more delicious, more savory and more ethereal than if they had come from the dish on the table.

And an evening without cakes and without pears from Papa's pockets was a sad evening for us.

I was the only one who really knew him, that simple heart, poetic and muted.

He earned, right up to the last expensive years, a modest twenty roubles or so. The small tips from buyers were scarcely enough to increase his budget. And yet my father had not been a poor young man.

The photograph of him in his youth and my own observations of our wardrobe proved to me that when he married my mother he had a certain physical and financial authority; for he presented his fiancée—a little girl who grew after her marriage—with a magnificent shawl.

Once married, he gave up turning over his wages to his father and supported his own household.

5 But first I'd like to finish the silhouette of my bearded grandfather. I don't know how long he continued to teach. He was said to be a much-respected man.

Ten years ago, when I went to the cemetery with my grandmother to visit his grave and saw his monument, I was convinced that he was a good man. An inestimable man, a saint.

He lies close by the river near the dark fence where the troubled waters flow. Below the hill, near other saints long dead.

Though well worn, his gravestone, with the letters in Hebrew: "Here lies . . . ," is still intact.

My grandmother pointed to it.

"There is the grave of your grandfather, the father of your father and my first husband."

Her lips quivered, but she couldn't cry. She whispered a few words, her own or prayers. I heard her wailing as she bent over the monument, as though that stone and that little mound of earth were my grandfather, as though she were speaking to the bowels of the earth or as though the grave were a kind of cupboard with something shut away forever in it.

"I beseech you, David, pray for us. This is your Bachewa. Pray for your sick son, Chaty, for your weak Zussy, for their children. Pray that they may be upright, honest men before God and man."

On the other hand, I felt closer to my grandmother. All there was to that little old woman was a scarf around her head, a little skirt and a wrinkled face.

She was tiny.

6   In her heart, a love devoted to her few favorite children and to her book of prayers.

As a widow she married, with the approval of the rabbi, my other grandfather, my mother's father, himself a widower. My mother's mother and my father's father had died the year my parents married. My mother had ascended the throne.

2

I shall always have a sinking feeling in my heart—is it from sleep or from a sudden memory on the anniversary of her death?—when I visit her grave, the grave of my mother.

I seem to see you, Mama.

You come slowly towards me. So slowly that I want to help you. You smile my smile. Ah! that smile, mine.

My mother was born in Lyozno, where I painted the priest's house, the fence in front of the house and in front of the fence, the pigs.

Pope or no pope, he smiles as he passes by, his cross glistening; he is about to make the sign over me. His hand slides down along his hip. The pigs, like little puppies, run to meet him.

My mother was the eldest daughter of the grandfather who lay half his life on top of the stove, a fourth in the synagogue and the rest in the butcher shop. He rested so much that grandmother gave up and died in the prime of life.

That was when my grandfather began to stir. The way cows and cattle move.

Was my mother really so very short?

My father paid no attention to that when he married her. But that is a mistake.

In our eyes, our mother had a style that was rare, as rare as was possible in her workaday surroundings.

But I don't want to praise, to overpraise my mother who is no more! Can I speak of her at all?

Sometimes I would rather weep than speak.

At the cemetery, at the entrance, I rush forward. Lighter than a flame, than an airy shadow, I hasten to shed tears.

I see the river disappearing in the distance, the bridge farther off and, close at hand, the eternal barrier, the earth, the tomb.

Here is my soul. Look for me over here, here I am, here are my pictures, my origin. Sadness, sadness!

That is her portrait.

It does not matter. Am I not there myself? Who am I?

You will smile, you will be surprised, you are going to laugh, you passer-by.

Lake of sufferings, hair gray too soon, eyes—a city of tears, soul almost non-existent, brain that is no more.

What is there, then?

I see her managing the household, ordering my father about, always building little dream houses, setting up a grocery shop, supplying it with a whole wagonload of merchandise, without money, on credit. With what words, by what means can I show her smiling, seated for hours at a time in front of the door or at the table, waiting for some neighbor or other to whom, in her distress, she may unburden herself?

At night when the shop was closed and all of us children were home, Papa dozed off to sleep at the table, the lamp rested and the chairs grew bored; out-of-doors we couldn't tell where the sky was, where Nature had fled; not that we were silent, but simply that everything was quiescent. Mama sat in front of the tall stove, one hand on the table, the other on her stomach.

Her head rose to a point at the top where her hair was held in place by a pin.

She tapped one finger on the table that was covered with an oilcloth, tapped several times and that meant:

9 "Everyone is asleep. What children I have! I have no one to talk to."

She loved to talk. She fashioned words and presented them so well that her listener would smile in embarrassment.

Like a queen, erect, motionless, her pointed coiffure in place, she asked questions through closed lips that scarcely moved. But there was no one to answer her. At a distance I was the only one to follow her.

"My son," she said, "talk to me."

I am a little boy and Mama is a queen. What shall I say?

She is angry, her finger taps the table repeatedly.

And the house is enveloped in quiet sadness.

Friday, after the Sabbath dinner, when Father invariably fell asleep, always at the same time, the prayer unfinished (on my knees before you, Papa!), her eyes would become sad and she would say to her eight children:

"Children, let us sing the rabbi's song, help me!"

The children sang, the children fell asleep. She began to weep and I said:

"You're already beginning, so I shan't go on singing."

I wanted to say that my talent lay hidden somewhere in her, that through her everything had been passed on to me, everything except her spirit.

There! She is coming towards my room. (In the courtyard, at Javitch's house.)

She knocks and asks:

"My son, are you there? What are you doing? Was Bella with you? Do you want to eat?"

"Look, Mama, do you like it?"

10 She looks at my painting with God only knows what eyes!

I await the verdict. At last she says slowly:

"Yes, my son, I see; you have talent. But, my child, listen to me. Perhaps it would be better for you to be a clerk. I'm sorry for you. Where do you get that in our family?"

She was not only our mother, she was also a mother to her own sisters. If one of them was about to get married, my mother was the one to decide whether the fiancé was suitable. She it was who judged, investigated, asked questions. If the fiancé lived in another town, she went there and, as soon as she had learned his address, she would head for the store across the way, buy something and enter into conversation. And when night came, she would try to peer through the window into the fiancé's house.

So many years have gone by since she died!

Where are you now, dear little mother? In heaven, on earth? I am here, far from you. I would feel happier if I had been nearer you; at least I would have seen your monument, touched your tombstone.

Ah! Mama! I can't pray any more and I weep more and more rarely.

But my soul thinks of you, of myself, and my thoughts are consumed in grief.

I don't ask you to pray for me. You know yourself what sorrows I may have. Tell me, dear mother, from the other world, from Paradise, from the clouds, from wherever you are, does my love console you?

Can my words distill for you a little sweetness, tender and caressing?

3

Beside her, in the cemetery, lie other women from Mohileff or from Lyozno. Hearts at rest. I knew them. Always the same courage, as the result of which my rosy young grandmother died, worn out by work, while my grandfather spent his days in the synagogue or on the stove. The same marvelous courage after the fast on the Day of Atonement, in the dark of the moon, towards the New Year.

Dear young old man!

How I loved you when I was at Lyozno in your rooms that smelled of tanned cowhides! I loved your lambskins. Your entire wardrobe always hung in the entry, at the door, and the coat rack, with clothes, hats, whip and the rest made a definite silhouette, which I still haven't studied enough, against the gray background of the wall. All that was my grandfather.

In his stable there is a cow with a large belly; she is standing up and staring stubbornly.

Grandfather goes up to her and talks to her as follows:

"Eh, listen here! Give me your legs. I'll have to tie you up. We need goods, meat, you understand?"

She falls down with a sigh.

I stretch out my arms to caress her muzzle, to whisper a few words to her, that she mustn't worry, I'm not going to eat the meat; what more could I do?

She hears the wind in the rye and above the hedgerows she sees the blue sky.

But the butcher, in white and black, knife in hand, is rolling up his sleeves. Scarcely does one hear the prayer when, pushing back her head, he plunges the steel into her throat.

Streams of blood.

Unmoved, dogs and chickens wait for a drop of blood, a bit of meat that may fall to the ground.

All one hears is their clucking, their rustling and grandfather's sighs amid floods of fat and blood.

And you, little cow, naked and crucified, in heaven, you are dreaming. The glittering knife has borne you aloft.

Silence.

The intestines uncoil and pieces fall apart. The skin falls.

Pink pieces of flesh, reddened with blood, pour out. The steam rises.

What a profession in his hands!

I feel like eating meat.

Thus, every day, two or three cows are killed and the fresh meat is presented to the owner of the estate and to the other inhabitants.

My grandfather's house was filled for me with the sounds and smells of art.

It was only from the hides, hung up and drying like linen.

In the dark of night, it seemed to me that there were not only smells but a whole swarm of happiness, bursting the planks and flying off into space.

They slaughtered the cows cruelly. I forgave all. The hides dried piously, prayed loving prayers, implored the heavenly ceiling for the atonement of the sins of their murderers.

My grandmother always fed me with meat specially roasted, grilled or baked. What was it? I didn't know exactly. Perhaps the stomach, the neck, or the ribs, the liver, the lungs. I didn't know.

13　　　In those days, I was particularly stupid and, it seems to me, happy.

Grandfather, I still remember you.

One day, coming upon a sketch of a nude woman, he turned his back on it, as if it were none of his business, or as if it were a strange star in the market place of no concern to the inhabitants.

And I understood then that my grandfather, as well as my wrinkled little grandmother and all my family, completely ignored my art (what an art, that doesn't even pretend to a resemblance!) and valued meat very highly.

This is what my mother told me about her father, my grandfather from Lyozno. Or perhaps I dreamt it.

The feast of Sukkoth or the feast of Simhath Torah.

They looked for him everywhere.

Where is he, where is he?

It turned out that, because of the fine weather, Grandfather had climbed up on the roof, had sat down on one of the chimney-pipes and was regaling himself with carrots. Not a bad picture.

It's all one to me if people are pleased and relieved to discover in those innocent adventures of my relatives the enigma of my pictures.

How little that interests me! My dear fellow-citizens, help yourselves!

If, for posterity, you lack proof of your rightness and my crime against common sense, I'll even tell you what my mother told me about my fine relations from Lyozno.

One of them could think of nothing better than to walk along the streets of the quarter, clad only in a shirt.

Well? Is that shocking?

The memory of that *sans-culotte* will always fill my

heart with radiant joy. As if a painting by Masaccio or by Piero della Francesca had come to life on the streets of Lyozno in broad daylight. He seemed so near to me.

But I'm not joking. If my art played no part in my family's life, their lives and their achievements greatly influenced my art.

You know, I was greatly excited as I stood beside my grandfather's seat in the synagogue.

Poor wretch, how I twisted and turned before I got there! Facing the window, my prayer book in my hands, I gazed at leisure on the sights of the quarter, on the Sabbath.

Beneath the drone of prayers, the sky seemed bluer to me. The houses float in space. And each passer-by stands out clearly.

Behind my back, they are beginning the prayer and my grandfather is asked to intone it before the altar. He prays, he sings, he repeats himself melodiously and begins over again. It is as though an oil mill were turning in my heart! Or as though a new honey, recently gathered, were trickling down inside me.

And, when he weeps, I remember my unsuccessful sketch and I think: Will I be a great artist?

I have forgotten to remember you, my little Uncle Neuch. With you, we used to go into the country to fetch cattle. How happy I was when you consented to take me with you in your jolting cart.

Somehow or other, we got along. To make up for it, there was always something to look at on every side.

Road, road, fine sandstone, and my Uncle Neuch sniffed and urged on his horse: "Eh, eh."

On the way back, I thought I ought to show more ingenuity and skill and I pulled the cow along by the tail, and begged her not to lag behind. As we crossed the wooden bridge, it seemed to me as if several wooden cutlets were rolling around in my stomach. The wheels sounded different.

My uncle never looked at the little river, the reeds, the fence along the bank, the mill or, farther on, the solitary little church, the tiny houses and the market place where everything was dark by the time we crossed it, tired out and I, God, or I cannot tell what, in my heart.

Everyone is buying and selling and behind the counter sit young girls.

I don't understand what it's all about.

I've just arrived and the girls are calling out to me from their shops and smiling at me. I have curly hair. They offer me buns, candies. Youth ripens in vain. Is it my fault? Can I divide myself?

It would be more interesting to paint my sisters and my brother.

How I would delight in the harmony of their hair, of their skin, how readily I would fling myself into them, intoxicating the canvases and you with the exuberance of my thousand-year colors.

But how describe them! I shan't try to say more than a word or two about my aunts, one of whom had a long nose, a good heart and ten children; the other, a shorter nose and half a dozen children, but she loved herself best,

I think—why not? The third, with a nose like a Morales painting, had three children, of whom one stuttered, one was deaf and the third still in the process of formation.

Aunt Mariassja is the palest.

Why then, frail as she is, does she live in this neighborhood?

In front of her house and shop the moujiks mill around.

Herring in barrels, oats, sugar shaped like pointed heads, flour, candles in blue wrappings—all that is for sale.

The money clinks.

Moujiks, tradesmen, men of God, whisper, stink.

My aunt lies on the sofa. Her yellow hands are folded, crossed. Nails black and white. Eyes white and yellow. Her teeth gleam faintly.

A black dress reveals her body, elongated, exhausted.

Her breasts sag and her stomach too.

Holy sounds reverberate beneath her feet.

Perhaps she will die soon and her body will contract in gentle ecstasy in the suburban earth.

More than once I have dreamed that a piece of buttered bun was falling from her hands into my mouth.

I stood at the door in front of her and, like a beggar, I gazed at the folds of that bun.

Aunt Relly is not like that at all.

Her little nose is like a pickle, her little hands and breasts are squeezed into her dark brown bodice.

She cackles, laughs, moves about, fidgets.

One skirt on top of the other, scarves below, above,

17 and her teeth fly towards her hair which is a tangled mass of combs and pins.

She brings out the thick fresh cream and invites me to taste the cheese.

Her husband is dead. Their tannery was shut down. All over the neighborhood the goats burst into tears.

And Aunts Moussia, Gouttja, Chaja!

On the wings of angels they flew across the market, over baskets of berries, pears and currants.

People look at them and ask:

"Who is flying like that?"

I have also had half a dozen or more uncles.

All of them were good Jews. Some of them with a bigger stomach and an emptier head, some with a black beard, others with a brown beard.

In short, this is painting.

Every Saturday Uncle Neuch put on a talis, any talis, and read the Bible aloud.

He played the violin like a cobbler.

Grandfather listened to him dreamily.

Rembrandt alone could have fathomed the thoughts of the old grandfather, butcher, tradesman and cantor, while his son played the violin before the window, before the dirty panes, covered with raindrops and finger marks.

Behind the window, the night.

Only the priest is asleep and behind him, behind his house, emptiness, ghosts.

But Uncle Neuch is playing the violin.

He who all day long leads the cows to the shed, ties

their legs and drags them around, is playing now, playing the rabbi's song.

It doesn't matter how he plays! I smile, sitting on his violin, jumping at his pockets, and pulling his nose.

He buzzes like a fly.

My head floats gently around the room by itself.

Transparent ceiling. Clouds and blue stars penetrate along with the smell of the fields, the stable and the roads.

I'm sleepy.

I'm content to pick up the crusts of bread, the spoon and to eat my supper, trembling.

Uncle Leiba is seated on a bench beside his country house. A lake. His daughters browse like red cows.

Uncle Judah is still on the stove.

He seldom goes out, not even to the synagogue.

He prays at home, before the window.

He moves his lips silently and his sallow complexion falls to the casement window, goes off down the street, lies down on the cupola of the church. He looks like a wooden house with a transparent roof.

I could have made a quick sketch of him.

Uncle Israel is still sitting in his same place in the synagogue, holding his arms behind him. He is warming himself, eyes closed, in front of the stove.

The lamp is lighted on the table. A shadow, dark and heavy, lies on the floor, on the altar.

He reads and sways to and fro, sways and sings, mutters and sighs.

Suddenly, he gets up.

"It's time to say the evening prayer."

It is night already! Blue stars. Violet earth.

19 The shops are closing.

Soon supper will be served—cheese, plates.

Why didn't I die in your house, under the table?

My uncle is afraid to offer me his hand. People say I'm a painter.

What if I should start to sketch him?

God does not permit it. A sin.

I have another uncle, Zussy; he's a hairdresser, the only hairdresser in Lyozno. He could be a hairdresser even in Paris. His manners, his mustache, his smile, his glance . . . He stayed in Lyozno. There, he was a star. Starred too was his window, the door of his shop. Above it a blue sign, showing a man wrapped in a white cloth, with soapy cheeks, and another shaving him—assassinating him.

Uncle Zussy cut my hair and shaved me with pitiless affection and boasted of me (he was the only one) throughout the entire neighborhood, even before the local squire.

When I painted his portrait and offered it to him, he glanced at the canvas, then, looking at himself in the mirror, thought a moment and said:

"Well, no! Keep it!"

God forgive me, if in my description I have not put that all-encompassing affection I have, in general, for all mankind.

And my parents are more saintly than the others.

That's the way I want it.

Green leaves rustling. Your stones. Your graves. Hedgerows, muddy river, prayers made. All that is before me.

20   No words. It all lies deep within me, writhes and soars like my memory of you.

Your pallor, the thinness of your hands, your dried skeletons, bring a lump to my throat.

To whom shall I pray?

How beseech you, beseech God through you, for a bit of happiness, of joy?

I often look at the emptiness of the blue sky, I look at it dry-eyed, with pity and sadness.

You know, my parents, I'm already a different man—sad and disillusioned of many things!

But enough! *Au revoir!*

4

Day after day, winter and summer, at six o'clock in the morning, my father got up and went off to the synagogue.

There he said his usual prayer for some dead man or other.

On his return he made ready the samovar, drank some tea and went to work.

Hellish work, the work of a galley-slave.

Why try to hide it? How tell about it?

No word will ever ease my father's lot (I beg of you, no compassion and certainly no pity, please).

There was always plenty of butter and cheese on our table.

Buttered bread, like an eternal symbol, was never out of my childish hands.

Wherever I went—to the courtyard, on the street and even to the toilet—I, like all the others, carried a slice of bread and butter.

Were we hungry? Not at all.

It was a sort of itch. A constant desire to eat, dream, yawn, chew something. In particular we liked to do . . . at night in the yard.

Excuse my vulgarity? Am I coarse?

It's only natural that, in the moonlight, when you're afraid to go too far—we children couldn't even budge, our legs simply wouldn't move.

The next morning Father would scold his children for their shameful conduct.

I liked to sleep. Not at night, in the morning I liked to sleep when a ray of sunlight peered at me through the window, from below the roof.

The flies are already buzzing about and rush towards your nose.

Oh! How long will it be?

Father comes in, a thin strap in his hand and speaks to me.

"It seems you have to go to school?"

I look at the blue curtains, the cobwebbed ceiling, the window framing the houses and I think:

"That's right, everyone seems to be up and about. Enough of scratching oneself!"

I hear the dining room door open. A woman comes in.

"Please give me three pennyworth of good herring. You ought to have some good herring."

I wake up. I don't know what time it is. It's morning. Tea is on the table. Impossible to convey its color, its smell. The sweetened liquid, followed by a bun, flows down inside me.

Fridays, the day my father takes a good wash. Mother piously brought the pitcher of hot water from the stove and Father washed here, there, his head, his chest, his black hands, groaning that nothing was ever in order, that there was no washing soda left.

"A whole family of eight children—on my hands! Not a bit of help!"

I swallowed my tears and thought of my poor art, of my future. The steam from the hot water, mingled with the smell of soap and crystals, overpowered me.

The candles, lighted in honor of the Sabbath, cut my throat the way that a cow's throat was cut in my grandfather's barn.

Sanctity of blood. It was warm and offensive.

The Sabbath dinner—father's clean hands, his face and his white shirt—calmed me. Everything was all right.

The meal was served. Oh! my appetite!

Stuffed fish, meat with carrots, noodles, calf's-foot jelly, meat broth, fruit compote, white bread. The temperature rose.

Father fell asleep.

I always looked at him jealously when he was served dishes of meat with sauce, particularly roasts.

How eagerly my eyes followed the casserole, from the place from whence it was taken, to where it was set down while Mother filled the plate.

Isn't there a tiny piece left, at least a little bone, which I, too, might enjoy?

Papa, tired, sad, ate, one would have said, with difficulty. His mustache moved up and down joylessly.

I watched him, like a dog. I wasn't the only one to watch.

Behind me and to the side, standing or sitting, were my younger sisters; a little farther off, my brother. All of us longed to eat roast in a pot like that! Delicious!

I thought: perhaps a time will come when I myself will be a father, master of the house and can eat such a roast whenever I please.

All those Sabbath dishes carried me far, far away, reminding me that life had a certain meaning.

The last piece of meat flies from Father's plate onto Mother's plate and back again.

"Eat it yourself."

"No, you eat it."

Papa was already snoring before he had time to say his prayer (what could one do?) and Mother was intoning the rabbi's song, before the stove, followed by all of us.

I remembered my grandfather, the cantor.

I remembered my mill-wheel and I sobbed to myself, farther away from the stove, behind the curtain, at the hem of my mother's dress.

She finished the song sobbing, in tears, in a loud voice, dragging out the words.

What heart (not mine) would not have burst that night at the thought that there was no one on the street, only the lamps leering and the riff-raff p. . . .

The candles burn down in the room, go out in the sky.

They smell strong. My head aches.

I'm afraid to go out in the courtyard.

One day, late in the evening, I met a thief there. She asked: "Where will I find a tavern in these parts? I've come from the cemetery."

Everyone is going to bed. But, from the direction of the market place, comes the distant sound of music in the park. People are strolling about there.

The trees caress one another, they bend down in the dark, the leaves murmur.

The night before Sabbath all of us children gathered around the table. But, during the week, Papa sat there alone, drinking his tea until ten o'clock at night.

My eldest sister, Aniouta, coming home from a walk, would go to fetch a herring from our store, which was at the entrance to the house, and carry it in by the tail. The younger girls, arriving later, each brought a herring in her turn.

Herring, pickles, cheese, butter and black bread, big and round, are on the table. The lamp barely lights all that. That is our dinner.

Sheer delight!

On weekdays I was fed, among other things, black kasha. To me there was no more devilish food than that.

The mere thought that the grains were in my mouth maddened me, as though my mouth were filled with buckshot.

In the days of the Soviets, however, I became a connoisseur of, and even grew to like, millet and barley meal —especially when a bag of it lay heavy on my back.

As a rule, towards dinner time, I'd fall asleep, fully dressed, and Mother would come to wake her first-born son.

"I don't know what's the matter with him; the minute dinner is ready, he falls asleep. My son, come and eat!"

"What?"

"Some gruel."

"Which kind?"

"Buckwheat with milk."

"I want to sleep, Mama."

"Come and eat first."

"I don't like it."

"Come on, just try; if it chokes you, if you faint, you needn't eat any more."

I confess that sometimes I fainted on purpose.

Now and then, they spared me. But that was in other days, other places and for other reasons.

Winter. My legs hold me upright, but my head is floating off. I huddle before the black cast-iron stove and warm myself.

26   In front, on a chair, my mother—broad, big-bellied—is seated like a queen.

Papa has put on the samovar and has begun to roll his cigarettes.

There's the sugar bowl! How glad I am!

Mama talks, talks, taps with her finger on the table, tosses back her hair.

Her tea grows cold. Papa listens to her, looks at his cigarette. A whole mountain of rolled cigarettes has already piled up.

Night.

Lying in my bed, I see on the wall a silhouette—a hand towel, perhaps. It looks to me like a ghost, a man, an uncle wearing a talis.

Suddenly he smiles. He turns threatening. Or else it's one or the other of my aunts or it's a ram.

I have to get up and go to my parents' bedroom, only as far as their door, for I'm afraid to go in there, especially when I see Father lying outstretched, beard in air, mouth open, snoring.

At the door I whisper:

"Mama, I'm afraid."

A voice, dreamily:

"What do you want?"

"I'm afraid."

"Go back to bed."

At once, I am calmed.

The little kerosene night-light gently takes possession of my soul and I walk slowly back to my bed where, at my feet, my brother David lies.

27 Poor David! Now that he lies in the Crimea, in its earth—still so young, he who loved me so dearly—his name is sweeter to me than a line of horizons and to me it breathes the perfume of my native land.

My brother! I could do nothing. Tubercular. The cypresses. Separated from us all. Decline.

But before that, we used to sleep together in the same bed.

At night I seemed to see the walls draw close.

The dim lamplight cast shadows on the ceiling. I hid my face in my pillow.

Suddenly I hear a mouse behind my head. Annoyed, I seize it noisily and fling it from me towards my brother's feet. Frightened in his turn, he flings it back at me. In the end we both go and drown it in the chamber-pot.

Already cool morning, blessed morning is coming through the windowpanes and we fall asleep.

When I was too frightened, my mother would call me to her.

That was the best shelter.

No hand towel will be changed into a ram and an old man, and no sepulchral figure will glide across the frozen windowpanes.

The drawing room mirror, tall and dark, will not frighten me any more.

In its corners and in the grooves of its frame are the souls of my parents, now long dead, the smiles of young girls.

Neither the hanging lamp nor the sofa will frighten me as long as I am in Mama's bed.

But I'm afraid. She is stout, with breasts as plump as pillows.

The softness of her body, from age and from bearing children, the sufferings of her maternal life, the sweetness of her workaday dreams, her legs fat and rubbery—I'm afraid of touching all that accidentally.

Our childhood illnesses usually began with dreams of my mother.

Night. The cold of winter. The house sleeps.

Suddenly, from the direction of the street, the silhouette of our dead Grandmother Chana closes the little *vasistas* with a bang, saying: "Daughter, why, in this cold weather, do you leave the window open?"

Or, another day, an old man, all in white, from the other world, comes to the house, an uncle with a long beard. Once inside, he remains standing, asks for charity. I offer him a piece of bread. Without a word, he strikes it. The bread falls.

"Chazia," said my mother, waking up. "Please go and take a look at the children."

That's the way we fell ill.

Sheds and roofs, beams, courtyards and all there was behind them, fascinated me.

And whatever was there, you may see it in my picture, "Above the Town." Or else, I can tell you about it.

A line of toilets, little houses, windows, gateways, chickens, a closed factory, a church, a little hill (old cemetery, no longer in use).

By crouching down low, I could see it more in detail from the little window in our attic.

I stuck my head outside and I breathed in the air, cool and blue. Birds fly past me.

I hear a housewife splashing around.

I see her stockings and her legs. She's dirtying my precious pieces of pottery I love so much, my stones. She's hurrying to the wedding. She has no children.

There, she will weep over the fate of the fiancée.

I like wedding musicians, the sounds of their polkas and their waltzes.

I hurry too, and I weep there beside Mama. I like to weep a little when the badchan sings and cries in his high-pitched voice:

"Betrothed, betrothed! Think of what awaits you!"

What awaits you?

At those words my head detaches itself gently from my body and weeps somewhere near the kitchens where the fish is being prepared.

No more weeping! Enough of that!

People blow their noses and confetti rises in clouds, little bits of multi-colored papers.

Congratulations! Good luck!

Grandfathers and grandmothers, young girls and young men, beggars and musicians, we all prance around, clap and cross hands.

We kiss each other, we sing, we dance, we go round in a circle.

"Congratulations!"

And I, whom shall I kiss?

I'll have to find someone. After all, I can't kiss an old woman, a bearded man.

I'm looking for some beauty or other.

Alongside our house were others in which the inhabitants came and went busily.

Behind us lived a carter.

He worked at the same time as his horse. His good horse hauled the loads as best he could. But it was really the carter who hauled him.

He was tall and thin, taller than his horse, longer than his cart.

When he sat on top of it and held the reins and the whip in his hands, he looked as though he were sailing a boat. But there was no wind.

On the contrary. It was calm and pleasant outside.

He didn't earn his living. His wife sold brandy at home (illegally), but it was the husband who drank all the liquor secretly, all by himself.

Then that was the end of quiet on our street. He didn't know how to sing. Drunk, he could only whinny in front of his horse. Surely that horse must have laughed.

But the carter, forgetting his horse, would stagger along beside the cart.

Opposite us, and just barely visible, was another little house.

There Tanjka, a laundress and a thief, lived: in the other half of the house, a chimney sweep with his wife and numerous progeny.

All one ever heard was their quarreling.

Voices came out of the stovepipe near which stood a pail of water in case of fire.

Now and then, after the wife had insulted her husband to her heart's content, she would come outside for a breath of fresh air on the bench.

When I went out, too, at the same moment, she would nod her head, which meant:

"Eh! Well, what do you think of him, that blighter? And he still thinks he's right!"

On the left, another wooden house, in which lived a man and a boy.

They trafficked in horses. They also stole pigeons which they snitched in full flight, by driving them off their roosts.

Often, they fought on the street.

One day, I thought one of the men was even trying to carry *me* off, small as I was.

Crowded close beside the chimney sweep's lodging was the baker, the most distinguished family on our street.

From five o'clock in the morning, light burned in their window and their stove was already going. It was warm in the kitchen.

Baskets were quickly filled with good hot rolls, freshly baked. And, in the morning, I ran to fetch them gladly, carrying off proudly in my hands a couple of them, piping hot.

With what terror I looked at the little girls in our neighborhood! Youthful fury rose to such a pitch that the little girl, hypnotized, followed me into the courtyard where, after tormenting each other a little, we let each other go.

I don't remember now how old I was when, while playing with little Olga, I refused to give back her ball unless she showed me her leg.

"Show me your leg, up to there, and I'll give you back your ball."

Such indiscretions greatly astonish me today. And I'm annoyed at their lack of success. However, there were days when I didn't play only with sticks and dice and feathers, and when I stopped climbing around in nearby waste land with a playmate who pounded on the beams with his . . . , making my hair stand on end.

There were days I spent exclusively on the rafts. I bathed, put on my clothes, dove in again. However, I was a little embarrassed to go into the water. My school friend made fun of me.

"Oh! See what a little one he has!"

Nothing crushed me as much as such razzing from that red-headed rascal.

Always the same thing.

Has he any better than I, if he is a big idiot, a spoiled brat, debauched?

I'm alone in the river. I bathe. I scarcely disturb the water.

Around me, the peaceful town. The milky sky, dark blue, is a little bluer to the left and from above glows a divine happiness.

Suddenly, from the opposite bank, a puff of smoke pours out from under the roof of the synagogue.

As though you could hear the cries of the burning scrolls of the Torah and of the altar.

The windowpanes break.

Quick! Out of the water!

Stark naked, I run across the plank to get my clothes.

How I love fires!

33   Flames are bursting out on every side. Already half the sky is covered with smoke. It is reflected in the water.

The shops close.

Everyone and everything is in motion—people, horses, furniture.

Cries, shouts, heavy falls.

Dearer to me now, more affecting, the house where I was born.

I run towards it, to look at it, to say good-bye to it.

Live sparks, cinders, shadows, are already falling on the roof.

It's as though it was vanishing.

My father and I, the neighbors, pour water on it, soak it; we save it.

Towards evening, I climb up on the roof to get a better look at the burned town.

Everything is smoking, cracking, collapsing.

Sad and weary, I go back into the house.

5

In addition to my skill at battledore and shuttlecock, at bathing and standing on roofs during fires, I had other talents.

Haven't you heard my childish voice at Vitebsk?

In our courtyard there lived an old man, short and fairly stout.

His long black beard, lightly flecked with silver, moved continually, now jutting up in the air, now pointing down to the ground.

He was a teacher and a cantor.

Not too impressive either as teacher or as cantor.

I took rudimentary lessons and also singing from him.

Why did I sing?

Where did I learn that the voice is used not only for shouting and quarreling with one's sisters?

I had a voice and I raised it as often as I pleased.

On the street the passers-by would all turn round, but they did not realize this was singing. They would say to themselves:

"He's crazy! Well, what's he shouting about?"

I had agreed to act as helper to the cantor and, on holy days, to the whole synagogue, and I myself distinctly heard my sonorous soprano float upon the air.

I saw smiles, interested glances, on the faces of the faithful, and I dreamed:

"I'll be a singer, a cantor. I'll go to the Conservatory."

In our courtyard there also lived a violinist. I don't know where he came from.

During the day, he clerked for an ironmonger; in the evening he gave violin lessons.

I scraped out something.

And no matter what, or how, I played, he would always exclaim, beating time with his foot: "Admirable!"

And I thought: I'll be a violinist, I'll go to the Conservatory.

At Lyozno, in every house, our relatives, our neighbors, would invite me to dance with my sister. I was charming, with my curly hair.

I thought: I'll be a dancer, I'll go to . . . I didn't know where.

Night and day I wrote verses.

People spoke well of them.

I thought: I'll be a poet, I'll go to . . .

I no longer knew where to let myself go.

Have you ever seen our Dvina river in autumn days?

The bathing huts are taken down. No one bathes any more. It is cold.

Standing on the banks, the Jews cast their sins into the water. A boat is gliding along in the shade. You can hear the dip of the oars.

Way down deep in the water, head upside down, my father's reflection barely moves.

He, too, is casting the dust of sins from his garments.

On those holy days, they used to wake me at one or two o'clock in the morning and I would run off to sing in the synagogue. Why does one run like that in the gloomy night? I'd have been much better off in my bed.

In the dark, everyone was hurrying to the synagogue, driving away sleep. They will not go home to bed till they have finished the prayer.

The morning cup of tea with cakes the color and shape

of an Oriental relic, the banquet dishes carefully laid out and over which brief prayers floated before one could begin to eat.

The special dish for the Day of Atonement, the night before.

An evening of chickens, of bouillon.

Tall candles glow in the distance.

Soon they will be carried to the synagogue.

They are already on the way, those white candles, carefully trimmed, praying and beseeching.

They are the candles that shine for the dead, for my mother, my father, my brothers, my grandfather, for all those who lie beneath the earth.

Hundreds of candles glow, like flaming hyacinths, in boxes filled with earth.

They flare up high and blaze.

Faces, beards, white blotches, huddle close together, some standing, some sitting or bending over.

Before he goes to the temple, my father, stooped and out of breath, hunts out the book of prayers for my mother and, speaking directly to her, shows her the pages turned down.

"So then, from here, to there."

Sitting down at the table, he underlines the chosen passages with a pencil, with his nails.

In one corner, he writes: "Begin here."

Near a touching passage he notes: "Weep." At another: "Listen to the cantor."

And Mama went to the temple, assured that she would not shed tears uselessly, but only at the proper places.

If need be—if she lost the thread of the prayer—she

would look down from the height of the balcony where the women sat.

When coming to the sign "Weep," she would begin, like all the others, to shed divine tears. Their faces would redden and little moist diamonds would trickle down drop by drop, sliding over the pages.

Papa is all in white.

Once a year, on the Day of Atonement, he seems to me the prophet Elijah.

His face is a little more sallow than usual, brick-red after tears.

He wept naturally, silently and at the proper moments.

Not one excessive gesture.

Sometimes he would give a cry: Ah! Ah! as he turned to his neighbors to ask for silence during the prayer or for a pinch of tobacco.

As for me, I fled from the synagogue and ran towards the garden hedge. No sooner had I scaled it than I picked up a large green apple.

I took a bite of it, on that fast day.

Only the blue sky saw me, sinner that I was, and my teeth, chattering, consumed the juice and the core of the apple.

I simply could not fast to the end of that evening, in answer to Mama's question: "Did you fast?"

I replied, like one condemned: "Yes."

I have no words with which to describe the hours of prayer that evening.

At that hour, the temple seemed to me entirely peopled with saints.

Slowly, gravely, the Jews unfold their holy veils, filled

with the tears of all that day of prayers. Their garments spread out like fans. The clamor of their voices penetrates the ark, whose little portals are visible, not hidden.

I suffocate. I do not move.

Day without end! Take me, make me nearer to you! Say something, explain.

All day long I hear: Amen! Amen! and I see them all kneeling.

"If You exist, make me blue, fiery, lunar, hide me in the altar with the Torah! Do something, God, for our sake, for mine."

Our soul takes flight and, from beneath the colored windowpanes, arms are raised.

Outside, the dried branches of tall poplars sway peacefully.

In broad daylight little clouds form, break apart, melt into one another.

Soon the moon, a half-moon, will appear.

The candles have burnt down to the end and the tiny lights glow in the pure air.

Now the candles reach up towards the moon, now the moon comes flying down towards our arms.

The very road prays. The houses weep.

And over all stretches the sky.

The stars come out and fresh air enters your opened mouth.

Thus we go back home.

What evening is lighter, what night more transparent than today's?

Papa goes to bed, tired, hungry.

His sins are already forgiven and Mama's too. Alone, I myself perhaps remain slightly a sinner.

And Passover! Neither unleavened bread, nor horse-radish, nothing excites me as much as the Haggadah, its lines, its pictures and the red wine in full glasses. I should like to have drained all the glasses.

Impossible.

Sometimes the wine in Papa's glass seemed to me even redder.

In its reflections, deep purple, royal, the ghetto marked out for the Jewish people and the burning heat of the Arabian desert, crossed with so much suffering.

And the night light, streaming down from the hanging lamp—how it weighs on me!

It seemed to me I saw tents on the sands; Jews, naked under the burning sun, arguing violently about us, about our existence—Moses and God.

My father, raising his glass, tells me to go and open the door.

Open the door, the outside door, at such a late hour, to let in the prophet Elijah?

A cluster of white stars, silvered against the background of the blue velvet sky, force their way into my eyes and into my heart.

But where is Elijah and his white chariot?

Is he still lingering in the courtyard to enter the house in the guise of a sickly old man, a stooped beggar, with a sack on his back and a cane in his hand?

"Here I am. Where is my glass of wine?"

In summer, when the children of the rich went on vacation, my mother would say to me pityingly:

"Listen to me, son, if you wish, go to Lyozno to visit Grandfather for a fortnight."

40   A suburb, just as in the pictures.

Once more, there I am.

All the houses are there, as well as the little river, the bridge, the road. It's all there. And the massive white church is there too, in the center of the great square.

Round about it, the inhabitants are selling sunflower seeds, flour, crockery.

The moujik, on his cart, drives casually into the quarter as if he just happened to be passing through. He goes toward one door or another.

An Oriental merchant or his ever-pregnant wife follow him, making fun of him:

"The devil take you, Ivan! Don't you know me? Don't you need anything today?"

On market days, the little church suffocates, crammed with people.

Moujiks on their carts, baskets, all sorts of wares pack it so tight that it seems as though God Himself has been driven out of it.

On every side people milled, shouted, stank. Cats meowed. Roosters for sale cackled, tied up in their baskets. Pigs grunted. Mares neighed.

Brilliant colors whirled about in the sky.

But towards evening, everything was quiet.

The icons came to life, the watch-lights glowed again. The cows fell asleep in their barns, snoring in the manure and so, too, did the hens on the rafters, blinking their eyes maliciously.

The tradesmen are already at the table under the lamp, adding up their accounts. Girls with plump, milky breasts languish in the corners.

41   Try to squeeze them. A white, sugary liquid will spurt out over your cheeks.

The white moon, bewitched, turns round behind the roofs and only I, dreaming, remain on the square.

Before me a transparent pig ecstatically buries its feet in the mud.

I'm on the street. The posts slant.

The sky is grayish-blue. The trees, wide-spread, bend down.

How I wish I could ride a horse!

But that animal of my grandfather's isn't a horse. It's an old crock, with a long neck.

I beg Uncle Neuch:

"Dear uncle, I want . . . I'd so much like to . . ."

"What?"

"To ride the old nag."

"But you don't know how, you couldn't."

"Oh, yes, I do . . ."

The old nag stands before me, head lowered.

She is sad. Her lips work.

She smiles, perhaps at the grass.

At last I mount her, I climb up on her back, no saddle, no anything and, you know, her belly is huge.

My feet are spread wide apart, my arms are up in the air.

But the old nag is already off. I'm carried away, toppled over onto the ground. I expect to be kicked by her hoofs. But she runs off joyously, with all her strength, towards the open fields.

We hunt for her all afternoon.

42   Uncle Neuch scolds me. Where is that mare?

Far away, in the forest, we shall find her staggering along, her little bell tinkling.

Quietly munching grass.

6

However, the years were passing. I had to begin to imitate others, to be like them.

And one fine day I saw before me a teacher, a little rabbi from Mohileff.

As if he had jumped out of my picture, or had run away from a circus.

We hadn't even sent for him. He came of his own accord, the way the marriage-broker comes or the old man who carries away corpses.

"One season, two . . ." he said to my mother.

How glib he is!

I look him straight in the face.

I already know that 'a' with a line below it makes 'o.' But at the 'a,' I fall asleep; at the line I would like . . . And exactly at that moment the rabbi falls asleep too.

How funny he is!

With the promptness of a thunderbolt I entered his class, and every night, a lantern in my hand, I went back home.

On Fridays he took me to the baths and made me stretch out on a bench.

Birch-rods in hand, he examined my body closely, as if I were the Bible.

I have had three rabbis like that.

The first, a little bedbug from Mohileff.

The second, Rabbi Ohre (a nonentity, no memory of him).

The third, an imposing person, who died too young, Rabbi Djatkine.

He was the one who taught me that famous speech

44   about tefillin which, when I had attained my thirteenth year, I recited standing on a chair.

I admit I considered it my duty to forget it less than an hour later, or even sooner.

I think my first little rabbi from Mohileff had the greatest influence on me.

Just imagine! Every Saturday, instead of going bathing in the river, my mother sent me to him to study the Bible.

However, I knew that at that hour (immediately after lunch) the rabbi and his wife, completely undressed, slept soundly in honor of the Sabbath. Well then, let's wait till he puts on his pants!

Once, knocking at the closed door, I aroused the attention of the master's dog, a reddish-brown mongrel, old and bad-tempered, with sharp teeth.

Quietly he crept down the staircase and, pointing his ears, came towards me and . . .

I've forgotten what happened after that. I remember being picked up at the great entrance door.

My arm bleeding, my leg also.

The dog had bitten me.

"Don't undress me, just put some ice on here . . ."

"We must carry him to his mother's as quickly as possible."

That same day the dog was hunted by the police and not till they had fired twelve bullets did they kill him.

That night, accompanied by my uncle, I set out for Petersburg to seek medical attention.

The doctors said I would die in four days.

Charming! Everybody takes care of me. Each day brings me closer to death. I'm a hero.

ראבקין דער
מעלאמד

45   The dog was mad.

The idea of going to Petersburg for treatment was very alluring to me.

It seemed to me I would meet the Czar on the street.

Passing the Neva, I had the impression that its bridge was suspended from the sky.

I forgot the dog bite. It was a pleasure to lie alone in a white bed, to have yellow bouillon, with an egg, for breakfast.

It was a pleasure to walk in the hospital garden; among the well-dressed children playing there I thought I saw the Crown Prince. I kept to myself, I did not have a good time, I had no toys. I saw so many toys, and such beautiful ones, for the first time.

They had never bought me any at home.

The uncle who had come with me advised me to quietly take one of the abandoned toys. An adorable toy, which worried me much more than my arm bitten by a mad dog.

But won't the little prince come back and take it from me?

The nurses smiled at me. Their smile encouraged me. But I always seemed to hear the child, the owner of the stolen toy, weeping.

At last I recovered and went home.

I found the house full of women decked out in their best clothes, and grave men, whose dark spots of color veiled the light of day.

Noise, whispering; all of a sudden, the piercing wail of a newborn babe.

Mama, half naked, pale, with a faint pink flush on

her cheeks, is in bed. My younger brother had just been born.

Tables covered in white.

The rustle of holy garments.

An old man, murmuring the prayer, cuts with a sharp knife the little bit of skin below the newborn babe's belly. He sucks the blood with his lips and stifles the babe's cries and moans with his beard.

I am sad. Silently, beside the others, I munch pastry, herring, honey-cake.

As each year passed I felt myself moving towards unknown thresholds. Especially from the day when my father, wearing the talis, recited above my boyish, thirteen-year-old body, the prayer of the transfer of moral responsibility. What should I do?

Remain an innocent child?

Pray morning and evening and everywhere I go, whatever I put in my mouth and whatever I hear, immediately say a prayer? Or flee from the synagogue and, throwing away the books, the holy vestments, roam the streets towards the river?

I was afraid of my majority, afraid of having, in my turn, all the signs of the adult man, even the beard.

In those sad, solitary days, those thoughts made me weep towards nightfall, as though someone were beating me or announcing the death of my parents.

Through the half-opened door I looked into our large and gloomy drawing room. There was no one in it. The mirror, alone and cold, swinging free on its stand, shone with a strange light.

47 I rarely looked at myself in it. I was afraid of being caught—in the act of admiring myself.

Nose long at the nostrils, alas! Broad, sharp cheekbones, irregular profile.

Sometimes I would stand and gaze at myself thoughtfully.

What is the meaning of my youth?

I'm growing up in vain. Useless and fleeting beauty immobilized in the mirror.

Once I have reached the age of thirteen, my carefree childhood will be over and all the sins will fall on my head. Shall I sin?

I burst into loud laughter and my white teeth flash in the mirror.

One day my mother drags me to the elementary school. Looking at it from the outside I had thought:

"I'll certainly be sick to my stomach here and the professor won't let me go outside."

It's true, the cockade is alluring.

They'll put it on my cap, and if an officer passes, won't I have to salute him?

Officials, soldiers, policemen, schoolboys—aren't we all alike?

But in that school, they don't take Jews. Without a moment's hesitation, my courageous mother walks up to a professor.

Our Savior, the only one with whom we can come to terms. Fifty roubles, that's not much. I enter directly into the third form, solely because that is his class.

With the school cap on my head, I began to eye the open windows of the girls' school more boldly.

I wore a black uniform.

My body rebelled. And I surely became more stupid than ever.

The professors are in blue tailcoats, with gilt buttons.

How many thoughts raced through my head as I gazed at them! How much they knew!

Where do they come from, what do they want?

I looked at Nicolas Efimowitch's eyes, at his back and at his blond beard.

I couldn't forget that he was the one who had accepted the bribe.

The other, Nicolas Antonowitch, an impeccable scholar, strode up and down the classroom and, though he read reactionary newspapers, he was much closer to me.

I didn't always understand the sort of remarks he made to certain pupils.

After gazing at a pupil a long time, he would look him in the eye and ask:

"Again, Volodia?"

Again—what?

Days passed before I understood the meaning of that "again."

Then why did all the others blush except me?

Back in the classroom I asked a comrade to explain what Nicolas Antonowitch was accusing Volodia of.

Smiling, he replied:

"You fool! Don't you know Volodia is an on . . . ?"

Nevertheless I still didn't know what he meant. The other boy laughed.

My God! The whole world was changed for me and I was sad.

49   I don't know why, but at that time I began to stammer (a strike, or something?)

Though I knew my lessons perfectly, I refused to recite them. It was funny, but rather tragic.

To hell with zeros!

The sea of heads on all those benches upset me completely.

I began to tremble distressingly and when I went up to the blackboard, I turned as black as soot and as red as a boiled lobster.

It would be over. Sometimes I even smiled.

That was the ecstasy of my shock.

Of course they prompted me from the first benches—but it was no use! And yet I knew my lesson. But I stammered.

I felt as if a reddish dog had run up and was barking over my prostrate body. My mouth was full of dust. My teeth hardly looked white at all.

What was the good of those lessons?

One hundred, two hundred, three hundred pages of my books I would have torn out ruthlessly, scattered to the four winds.

Let them whisper in the air to each other all the words of the Russian language, all the words of all the countries and all the seas!

Let me alone!

I want to stay wild, untamed, to cover myself with green leaves, to shout, weep, pray.

"Come, Chagall," says the professor, "are you going to recite your lessons today?"

I begin: "Ta . . . ta . . . ta . . ."

I thought they would throw me from the top of the fourth floor!

Life in uniform trembled like an autumn leaf.

But in the end, I went back to my seat.

In the distance, the professor's hand drew a very distinct "two."

I could still see that.

Through the classroom windows I saw trees, the school for young girls.

"Nicolas Antonowitch, may I be excused?" I say. "I have to go."

I had one thought only: when will I be through with my classes, will I have to go on much longer, and couldn't I leave without completing the course?

On days when I wasn't called to the blackboard, when all the pupils were in an uproar, I really didn't know what to do.

Rooted to my desk, pinched and prodded from every side, I didn't know where to turn. I twisted and squirmed, rocked back and forth, got up and sat down.

All of a sudden, I put my head out of the window to throw a kiss to a pretty stranger.

The inspector comes towards me. He grabs my hand, raises it.

Caught! I turn red, pink, white!

"Remind me tomorrow, you rascal, to give you a 'two' for conduct." It was at this time that I revelled in drawing. I did not know what that portended.

My sketches flew over our heads, often even hitting the professor's.

S . . ., the boy next to me, indulging in his favorite pastime, thumped under the bench with . . .

A muffled sound which, sometimes, attracted the professor's attention.

Everyone keeps still. Everyone laughs.

"Skorikoff!" the professor calls out. S . . . gets up, blushes and, having received his "two," sits down again.

What I liked best was geometry. At that I was unbeatable. Lines, angles, triangles, squares carried me far away to enchanting horizons. And during those hours of drawing, I lacked only a throne.

I was the center of the class, the object of attention and an example for all.

I did not come to myself till the next lesson.

At the end of the year, after fencing with singlesticks and doing special exercises with the twenty-kilo weight, I was obliged to stay in the same form a second term.

What happened after that, I've forgotten.

No matter! What's the use of being in a hurry?

I had plenty of time to become a clerk or an accountant. Let time pass, let it drag along!

Once again I'll stay up late at night, hands in my pockets, looking as if I were studying. Again I'll hear Mama call from her bedroom:

"You've burnt enough oil! Go to bed. Haven't I told you to do your lessons in the daytime? You're crazy! Let me sleep!"

"But I'm not making any noise!" I'll say.

I look at my book, but I think of the men who, at this moment, are walking along the streets, I think of my river, of the floating rafts, bumping about at the end of the bridge, sometimes breaking up against it.

The planks crack, rise up in the air, but the rowers escape . . .

Why don't they fall in too?

It would be interesting to see them wrecked that way.

I think, too, of that stout gentleman, with the puffy cheeks, who walks across the bridge, ogling young girls. At the café he swallows half a dozen cakes at one gulp. He is big and fat, and he thinks he's very intelligent.

At the library he chooses the most serious newspapers. He reads them, puffing and blowing his nose with a thousand apologies.

One day at the tailor's, brandishing his cane, proud of his youthful plumpness, he asks the tailor, the latter's assistant and even the boy:

"Excuse me, sir, but please tell me how much cloth would I need for a sensible pair of trousers?"

Fool, windbag, bonehead, ass!

When I was in the fifth form, this is what happened to me in the drawing lesson. An old-timer of the front row, the same boy who pinched me the most often, suddenly showed me a sketch on tissue paper, copied from the magazine *Niwa*: The Smoker.

In the midst of confusion! Let me be!

I don't remember exactly, but that drawing which was not done by me, but by that fathead, threw me into a towering rage.

It roused a hyena in me.

I ran to the library, grabbed that enormous volume of *Niwa* and began to copy the portrait of the composer, Rubinstein, fascinated by his crow's-feet and his wrinkles, or by a Greek woman and other illustrations; perhaps, too, I improvised on it.

All that, I hung up in our bedroom.

I was familiar with all the street slang and with other, more modest, words in current use.

But a word as fantastic, as literary, as out of this world as the word "artist"—yes, perhaps I had heard it, but in my town no one ever pronounced it.

It was so far removed from us!

On my own initiative, I'd never have dared use that word.

One day a school friend came to see me and, after looking at our bedroom and noticing my sketches on the walls, he exclaimed:

"I say! You're a real artist, aren't you?"

"An artist? What's that? Who's an artist? Is it possible that . . . I, too . . .?"

He left without explaining.

I immediately remembered that somewhere in our town I had seen a large sign, rather like those signs on shops: Artist Penne's School of Painting and Design."

I thought: That does it. I've only to enter that school and I'll be an artist.

And, once and for all, I'll shatter my mother's illusions of making me a clerk or an accountant or, better still, a well-established photographer.

7

One fine day (but all days are fine!), as my mother was putting bread in the oven, I went up to her—she was holding the long-handled bread-pan—and, taking her by her flour-smeared elbow, I said to her:

"Mama . . . I want to be a painter.

"I'm through. I can't be a clerk, or an accountant. I'm sick of that. It's not for nothing I've had a feeling something was going to happen.

"You see, Mama, am I a man like other men?

"What am I fit for?

"I want to be a painter. Save me, Mama. Come with me. Come on, come on! There's a place in town; if I'm admitted and if I complete the courses, I'll come out a regular artist. I'd be so happy!"

"What? A painter? You're crazy, you are. Let me put my bread in the oven: don't bother me. My bread's all ready."

"Mama, I can't go on like this. Come on!"

"Don't bother me!"

At last, it is decided. We'll go to see Penne. And if he thinks I have talent, then we shall think about it. But if not. . .

(Nevertheless, I'm going to be a painter, I thought to myself, but by my own efforts.)

It's clear, my fate is in Penne's hands, at least as far as my mother, the ruler of our household, is concerned. My father gave me five roubles, the monthly price of the lessons, but he sent them rolling into the courtyard where I had to scramble after them.

I had discovered Penne at the very moment when, on the platform of the streetcar that ran down towards Cathedral Square, I had been dazzled by a white inscription on a blue background: "Penne's School of Painting."

Ah! I thought, what a clever town our Vitebsk is! I decided to make the acquaintance of the master.

That sign was actually only a large blue placard of sheet metal, exactly like those you can see everywhere on the front of shops.

As a matter of fact, in our town, small visiting cards, small plates on doors were useless. No one paid any attention to them.

"Gourevitch Bakery and Pastry Shop."

"Tobacco, All Brands."

"Fruit and Groceries."

"Warsaw Tailor."

"Paris Modes."

"Artist Penne's School of Painting and Design."

All that is business.

But that last placard seemed to me of another world. Its blue color is like the blue of the sky.

And it sways in sunshine and in rain.

After I'd rolled up my tattered sketches, I set out, trembling and excited, with my mother, for Penne's studio.

Even as I climbed his stairs, I was intoxicated with the smell of paints and paintings. Portraits on every side. The wife of the town's governor. The governor himself. Mr. L . . . and Madam L . . . , Baron K . . . with the Baroness, and many others. Did I know them?

Studio jammed with pictures, from floor to ceiling. On the floor, too, are piled stacks and rolls of paper. Only the ceiling is unencumbered. On the ceiling, cobwebs and absolute freedom. Stuck here and there are Greek plaster heads, arms, legs, ornaments, white objects, all covered with dust.

I feel instinctively that this artist's method is not mine. I don't know what mine is. I haven't time to think about it.

The animation of the figures surprises me.

Is that possible?

As I climb the staircase, I touch noses, cheeks.

The master is not at home.

I shall say nothing of my mother's expression and her emotions on finding herself for the first time in an artist's studio.

Her eyes darted from corner to corner, she glanced two or three times towards the canvases.

Suddenly she turns to me and, almost imploringly, but in a firm, clear voice, says to me:

"Well, my son . . . you see: you'll never be able to do things like that. Let's go home."

"Wait, Mama!"

For my part, I've already decided that I'll never paint like that. Is it necessary?

There is something else. But what? I don't know.

We wait for the master. He must decide my fate.

My God! Suppose he's in a bad humor and cuts me off with a "That's no good."

(Everything is possible—prepare yourself, with Mama, or without her!)

No one in the studio. But in the other room someone is moving about. One of Penne's pupils, no doubt.

We go in. He scarcely notices us.

"How do you do!"

"How do you do!"

He is sitting astride a chair, painting a study. I like that.

Mama immediately asks him a question:

"Tell me, please, Mr. S . . . what about painting? Is there anything in it?

"Well . . . nothing special . . ."

Naturally one couldn't expect a less cynical, less vulgar, reply.

It was enough, however, to convince my mother she was right and to instill in me, stammering youngster, a few drops of bitterness.

But here is the master.

I would be lacking in talent if I could not describe him to you. It did not matter that he is short. His silhouette is none the less friendly.

The tails of his jacket hang in points towards his legs.

They float to right, to left, up, down and, at the same time his watch-chain follows them. His blond goatee, pointed and mobile, expresses now melancholy, now a compliment, a greeting.

We step forward. He bows negligently (one bows with precision only to the governor of the town and to the rich).

"What can I do for you?"

"Well, I don't know . . . he wants to be a painter . . . He's crazy, he is! Please look at his drawings . . . If he has any talent, it would be worth while to take lessons, but if he hasn't . . . Come, my son, we're going home."

Penne did not bat an eye.

(You wretch, I thought, come, give us a sign).

He thumbs mechanically through my copies of *Niwa* and mutters:

"Yes . . . he has some ability . . ."

Oh! You . . . I thought to myself.

To be sure, my mother didn't know any more than she had before.

But, for me, that was all I needed to hear.

My father gave me a number of five-rouble pieces and I studied for barely two months, in the Penne school at Vitebsk.

What did I do there? I don't know.

A plaster model was hung up in front of me. I had to draw it at the same time as the other pupils.

I set myself to my task studiously.

I held my pencil up to my eyes, I measured, measured. Never just right.

Voltaire's nose always bends down.

Penne comes up to me.

The shop next door sold paints. I had a small box and the tubes dangled in it like children's corpses.

No money. To get subjects for studies I went to the far end of the town. And the farther I went, the more frightened I became.

In my fear of crossing "the frontier" and finding myself close to army camps, my colors became dingy, my painting turned sour.

Where are those studies on huge canvases that hung above Mama's bed: water carriers, little houses, lanterns, processions on the hills?

It seems that as the canvases were heavy and thick, they had been used on the floor as carpets.

59   A nasty idea!

People must wipe their feet. The floors have just been washed.

My sisters thought pictures were made expressly for that purpose, particularly when painted on large canvases.

I sighed and came within an ace of strangling myself.

In tears, I picked up my canvases and hung them again at the door, but, in the end, they were carried off to the attic where they were gradually covered with dust and dirt and sank down peacefully in it forever.

At Penne's I was the only one who painted with violet. What's that?

How does that happen?

It seemed so daring that after that I attended his school free of charge until, for me, it became—to use S.'s expression—nothing special. The environs of Vitebsk. Penne.

The earth in which my parents sleep—all that is left today of what was most dear to me.

I like Penne. I see his wavering silhouette.

Like my father, he lives in my memory. Often, when I think of the deserted streets of my town, I see him now here, now there.

More than once, in front of his door, on the threshold of his house, I longed to plead with him:

I don't want fame, but only to be a silent worker like you; I want to be hung, like your paintings, in your street, near you, in your house. May I?

8

I have forgotten the names of those holiday eves when, one by one or in groups, the Jews go to the cemetery.

After an hour or two, wormwood plants appear on the street, like a naked body among people in clothes.

I take my books and I, too, go there. I arrive and I sit down. I touch the hedges. Is this sad?

We two know how sweet it is to roam about those sleeply places. Nothing lives there any more, nothing stirs. Our feet brush against bits of paper, notices, odd bits of letters, and those who wrote them are themselves lying here somewhere. The dry grass at the foot of graves: footprints, porous, damp, disappear. The tomblike earth drinks tears and each of the dead suffocates and dies a second time. One must not weep on graves. One must not lie down on the graves of children.

Long, long ago the marble slab on the grave of my little sister, Rachel, disappeared. She wasted away as the result of eating charcoal. At last, pale and thin, she breathed her last sigh. Her eyes filled with the blue of heaven, with dark silver. Her pupils became fixed. Flies hovered around her nostrils. No one drove them away.

I got up from my chair, drove them away and sat down again. I got up again and I sat down again.

My eyes were scarcely wet when I saw the candles lighted at the head of her bed. An old man stood by her side, guarding her all night long.

And to think that, in a few hours, that little body will be lowered into the earth and men's feet will trample on it!

No one gives a thought to dinner. My sisters have hidden behind the curtains at the door; they weep, press their ten fingers to their mouths and dry their tears with their hair and their blouses.

I couldn't understand how a living being can die all of a sudden.

I had often seen people buried, but I wanted to see the one that was in the coffin. I was afraid of it, too.

Suddenly, one morning, well before dawn, shouts rose from the street below our windows. By the faint light from the night-lamp, I managed to make out a woman, alone, running through the deserted streets.

She is waving her arms, sobbing, imploring the inhabitants, still asleep, to come and save her husband, as if I or the big-bellied cousin dozing in her bed, could cure, could save a dying man. She runs on.

She's afraid to stay alone with her husband.

People, alarmed, come running from every side.

Everyone talks, gives advice, rubs the sick man's arms, his oppressed chest.

They spray him with camphor, alcohol, vinegar.

Everyone groans, weeps.

But the steadiest, inured to sorrows, push the women aside, calmly light the candles and, in the silence, begin to pray aloud over the dying man's head.

The light from the yellow candles, the color of that face, barely dead, the assured movements of the old men, their impassive eyes, convince me—and those around me —that it's all over.

The rest of you can go back to your houses now, go and lie down again or light the samovar and open the shops.

All day long we shall hear the lamentations of children singing "the Song of Songs."

The dead man, solemnly sad, is already laid out on the floor, his face illumined by six candles.

In the end, they carry him away.

Our street is no longer the same. I don't recognize it any more than I do those women who howl wildly.

A black horse hauls the coffin.

He is the only one to do his duty without any fuss; he is taking the dead man to the cemetery.

One day a pupil of Penne's came to my house, the son of a big merchant and a former classmate from the elementary school, which he had left for a more bourgeois school, a business school. His particular merits caused him to be invited to leave that one in turn.

Black hair, a pale face, he was as foreign to me as his family was to mine.

When he met me on our bridge, he never failed to stop and question me, blushing, about the color of the sky or the clouds and he asked me to give him lessons.

"Don't you think," he said to me, "that that cloud, down there near the river, is intensely blue? Where it is mirrored in the water it turns to violet. Like me, you adore violet. Don't you?"

I controlled the emotions that had been building up in me ever since my studies in that elementary school, where that aristocrat used to look at me as if I were some sort of curiosity.

That boy had a rather pleasant face and I was often at a loss to know with what to compare it.

Ignoring the wealth and ease that surrounded him, he enriched my childhood years.

"All right," I said to him, "I'll be your teacher, but I don't want any money from you. Let's rather be friends."

More and more I deserted my home to spend all my days with him in his house in the country.

What is the use of writing all that? Because the distinction of my friends was the only thing that gave me a little courage to hope to become more than the humble lad from Pokrowskaja Street.

He had traveled and he told me he was getting ready to leave for Petersburg to continue his art studies there.

"I say, why don't we go together?"

What could I do, the son of a simple clerk? I had already been apprenticed to a photographer. He predicted a splendid future for me, provided I was punctual and agreed to work for him gratis for another year.

"Art," said he, "is a fine thing, but it won't run away from you! And besides, what good is it? Just see what a fine setup I have! Nice apartment, fine furniture, customers, wife, children, the respect of all—you'll have all that too. You'd better stay with me."

He was a dyed-in-the-wool bourgeois, always particular about his appearance. How many times I had a wild desire to throw his photos to the winds and skip out!

I hated the work of retouching. And I never succeeded in mastering it. I saw no need of filling in those lines, wrinkles and crow's-feet, of rejuvenating faces so that they looked different, never natural.

When I came across the picture of an acquaintance, I smiled at him. I was ready to improve that one!

I remember how my mother went to have her photograph taken for the first time.

On both sides of the photographer's sign were medals. Imagine our excitement!

To save expense, our whole family, uncles and aunts included, decided to have themselves photographed together on one little card.

I, a little lad of five or six, dressed in a suit of red velours with gilt buttons, stood close to my mother's skirts. Like my sister, who stood on her other side, I had my mouth open—the better to breathe.

When we went to fetch the proofs, we bargained a little, as was customary.

The photographer flew into a rage and tore the only sample of the photograph to bits.

I was stunned; nevertheless I picked up the scattered pieces and once home I glued them together again.

Thank God!

Another photographer, with whom I worked, was much nicer. He groaned so loudly he could be heard in the next room.

At least he paid me by feeding me. I shall never forget the soups, the large portions of meat they gave me as well as the other workers. And as much bread as I wanted.

Thank you!

All of a sudden, something snaps.

Armed with my twenty-seven roubles, the only ones I received from my father in my life (for my art tuition)— I flee, still pink-cheeked and curly-haired, to Petersburg, followed by my old schoolmate. The die is cast.

With how many tears and with what pride I gathered up that money my father had flung under the table (I forgive him, it was his way of giving). I stooped down and picked it up.

On my knees under the table, I thought of future nights when I would be hungry and alone on streets filled with well-fed people.

Only I, a little fellow, would want to eat, to have some place to sleep. At that moment I thought it mightn't be so bad to stay there under the table.

In answer to my father's questions, I stammered that I wanted to enter a school of a . . . a . . . a . . . art.

I don't recall my father's reply or his grimace.

He immediately rushed off, as usual, to set the samovar boiling, and as he walked away, he flung at me:

"Well then, go if you wish. But I want to tell you one thing—I haven't any money. You can see for yourself. That's all I've been able to scrape together. Impossible to send you anything. Don't count on it."

It doesn't matter, I thought. With or without money, I'll go.

Is it possible that no one, anywhere, will give me a cup of tea? Is it possible I'll never find a piece of bread on a bench or on a post?

It often happens that people leave behind a piece of bread, wrapped in paper.

The essential thing is art, painting, a painting different from the painting everyone does.

But what sort? Will God, or somebody else, give me the power to breathe into my canvases my sigh, the sigh of prayer and of sadness, the prayer of salvation, of rebirth?

I recall that not a single day, not an hour passed now that I didn't tell myself: "I'm still a boy."

Terror gripped me; how could I manage to feed myself, since I'm good for nothing but perhaps to draw?

66   But to be a clerk, like my father—I couldn't do that either, for I hadn't the physical strength to lift huge barrels as he did.

I was even glad I had no choice but to become an artist. That was a good excuse not to be forced to earn my living. And certainly, being an artist, I thought, I'll become a man.

However, to live in Petersburg, one needs not only money, but also a special authorization. I am a Jew. And the Czar had set aside a certain residential zone in which the Jews were obliged to stay.

From a tradesman, my father obtained a provisional certificate as though I had been commissioned to go and fetch certain merchandise for him.

In 1907, I set out towards a new life, in a new city.

9

At the docks I courted the girls.

And in the yards, on rooftops, in garrets, I had a good time with my friends.

In front of our door, the noisy gossips of the house are sitting on a bench.

One of my friends passes. I hide behind the door and poke out my head.

"Joseph, tomorrow is examination day."

I'll spend the night at his house. I'll study his curly head.

"Let's do our work together."

Paykine and his toys, Jachnine and his herring, Matzenko and his locomotive, they all made me extremely uneasy.

But as long as I was playing in the courtyard, a slice of bread and butter in my hands, peace reigned in our house.

All was peaceful too when I studied at the elementary school and my little girl friends gave me presents of ribbons.

But as I grew up, I was overcome with fear.

It seems that my father, having in view certain privileges for my younger brother, had added two years to my age on my birth certificate.

My precocious adolescence. Night. The house sleeps. The porcelain stove is warm and glowing. Papa snores.

The street sleeps too, black and velvety.

Suddenly, outside, very close to our house, someone moves, blows his nose, whispers.

"Mama," I cry, "it must be the police come to take me off to the regiment."

"Quick, my son, hide under the bed."

I slide under and there I stay a long time, calm and happy.

You don't know how happy I am—and I don't know why—lying flat under the bed or on a roof, in some sort of hiding place.

Under the bed—dust, boots.

I lose myself deep in thought, I fly above the world.

But no policeman appears. I come out of hiding.

So then, I'm not a soldier? Still a little boy.

Thank God.

I go to bed again and I dream of policemen, soldiers, epaulettes, barracks.

However, in the days when I fenced with sticks, when I walked on roofs during the great fires, when I went bathing and drew pictures, nothing could stop me from paying assiduous court to the young girls on the embankments.

The sight of those schoolgirls, the lace of their long pantaloons, their plaits, tormented me.

Must I admit that, according to certain people and also the testimony of my mirror, the face of my precocious adolescence was a mixture of Passover wine, ivory-colored flour and faded rose petals that had strayed between the leaves of a book?

How I admired myself, you will say!

My intimates have surprised me more than once in front of the mirror. To tell the truth, I was looking at myself and thinking of the difficulties I should have if, one day, I should want to paint my portrait. However, there was also a bit of admiration in all that—why not? I admit,

69   I didn't hesitate to darken my eyes a little, to redden my lips lightly, though there was no need for it and yes, yes . . . I wanted to please those girls on the river side.

I was successful. But I was never able to profit from that success.

Here I am at Lyozno with Nina. A walk together that promises much: I sense it and I tremble. Or quite the opposite.

We are under the bridge, under the roof of an old garret, on a bench.

Night. We are alone.

In the distance, a cab rolls towards the station.

Not a person in sight. You can do what you please. And what do I please? I kiss her.

Once, twice. Today, tomorrow, there will always be a limit.

Soon dawn breaks. I'm annoyed. We go into her parents' house. The air there is stifling. Everyone is asleep.

Tomorrow is Saturday. And if they see me in the morning, they will all be pleased.

A very respectable fiancé. Everyone will congratulate us, Nina and me.

Shall I stay? What a night! How hot it is! Where are you?

I know nothing about the realities of making love. Didn't I sigh after Aniouta four years? And at the end of the fourth year all I dared do—and then only on her initiative—was to give her a startled kiss, one evening in front of the courtyard gate and just when her face was breaking out in pimples!

Two weeks later, I had stopped speaking to her. What

was the use? I'd learned that an actor was going around with her.

What scenes that passionate girl staged on purpose to lure me into the trap!

What intimate rendezvous she and her girlfriends slyly arranged!

I no longer knew what was happening to me or where my boldness had fled.

As a man, I was nothing. She understood that, and I knew it would have turned out quite differently if only I had been smarter.

No, no.

I was terrified by that corset she wore on purpose.

I didn't understand a thing and yet I realized I was wasting my time.

It was useless for her to go with me when I painted outside of town on the Jules hill. Neither the peace of the nearby forest, nor the deserted valleys, nor the vast fields, gave me the strength I would have needed to overcome my timidity and yet . . .

One evening I was sitting with her on the quay, at the far end of the town, near the baths.

Below, the river becomes shallow and flows gently.

"Take a chance!" I thought.

My cap is on her head. I lean against her shoulder. That's all.

Suddenly, I hear footsteps, a group of school friends are coming towards us.

They come near us, near me. I try to take back my cap.

"Aniouta, give me back my cap," I say.

We get up from the bench, but the cap is still on her head. The boys follow us.

Someone gives me a violent punch in the back, then shouts, as he runs off:

"Let her alone and don't you dare come back here again or else . . ."

Your face is no longer clear to me today, Aniouta.

It's a long time since all that happened.

I've grown up now; childhood and adolescence have long since left me and my head is full of so many sad thoughts.

How I should like to bring back those days again, to see your face, perhaps grown old now!

It was smooth then, without wrinkles, and once or twice I dared to kiss it. Do you remember?

You were the first girl to attract me and to kiss me. I was stunned, I couldn't speak. My head whirled. But I controlled myself and deliberately did not change expression to show you how sophisticated I was.

One day you fell ill. You were lying in your bed. There were little red pimples on your face. I went over to you and sat down on the foot of your bed. I asked you whether it was because I had kissed you the other night.

No, you said with a drawl, and you smiled.

Those days will never return.

On the skating rink, below the bridge, I was introduced to your friend Olga, a high-school student. Square face, nose slightly upturned, a trifle squint-eyed.

At sight of her I suffered the pains of a pregnant woman. All sorts of desires boiled up inside me, but she dreamed of a love that lasted forever.

I wanted to go off somewhere and forget all about her.

But I pitied her wasted hands and her legs that were rather short.

When I forsook her, I sent her a few farewell verses in which I assured her I was not made for the eternal love of which she dreamed.

With my third romance, I grew bolder. I kissed right and left. I didn't hold back any more.

Is it worth while to bore you, and myself, with a recital of my boyish romances?

Year after year, nights faded into dawn above me and behind fences and enclosures, love newly born died in vain.

In gardens and on paths, kisses have long since faded from the benches.

The rains have washed them away.

No one speaks your names any more.

I shall walk past your streets and I shall transfer the bitterness of dreary meetings to my canvases.

Let those mists of our days shine and flicker there.

And the spectator will smile.

I am at Thea's, lying on the sofa in the consulting room of her father, a physician. I liked to stretch out that way near the window on that sofa covered with a black horsehair cloth, worn, with holes in several places.

The same sofa, undoubtedly, on which the doctor examined pregnant women and sick people suffering from stomach, head or heart trouble.

I lay down on that sofa, arms above my head and,

dreaming, looked at the ceiling, the door, the place where Thea usually sat.

I'm waiting for her. She's busy. She's preparing dinner—fish, bread and butter—and her dog, big and heavy, keeps turning around her legs.

I lay down there on purpose so that Thea would come over to me, so she would kiss me. I held out my arms, the arms of salvation.

The bell rings. Who is that?

If it's her father, I'll have to get up from the sofa and go away.

Who is it then?

It's a friend of Thea's. She enters and I hear her voice, babbling away to Thea.

I stay in the consulting room. I don't leave. Yes, I did go out, but the friend, whose back was towards me, didn't see me.

I feel . . . what do I feel?

On the one hand, I'm annoyed at having my rest interfered with, my hope that Thea would perhaps come and sit beside me.

On the other, that young girl's visit and her voice, like that of a bird from some other world, trouble me.

Who is she? I'm afraid. No, I want to speak to her, to be near her.

But she's already saying good-bye to Thea. She scarcely glances at me and goes away.

Thea and I go out for a walk. On the bridge we meet her again. She is alone, all alone.

Suddenly I feel that I shouldn't be with Thea, I should be with her.

74   Her silence is mine. Her eyes, mine. I feel she has known me always, my childhood, my present life, my future; as if she were watching over me, divining my innermost being, though this is the first time I have seen her.

I knew this is she, my wife.

Her pale coloring, her eyes. How big and round and black they are! They are my eyes, my soul.

I knew that Thea was nothing to me, a stranger.

I have entered a new house and I cannot be parted from it.

10

The room at Javitch's, in our courtyard, was my studio. To reach it, you had to pass through the kitchen, the owner's dining room, where that huge, bearded old man, a leather merchant, sat at the table drinking his tea.

When I went through his room he would turn his head slightly: "Good day."

But I felt embarrassed when I saw the lamp on the table and two dishes on which lay an enormous bone.

His daughter, an ugly brunette, the perennial fiancée, smiled—a strange, wide smile. Her hair was like an icon's and her eyes shifted timidly.

When I appeared, she made a desperate effort to cover herself with a scarf or a napkin.

My room was lighted by the deep blue that fell through the solitary window. The light came from a distance: from the hill on which the church stood.

I always enjoy painting that church and that hill again in my pictures.

Many a time I jumped into my bed, feet in the air. Canvases on the walls, blurred windows, dirt, the solitary chair and rough table.

Bella knocks at the door, she knocks timidly with her thin, slender little finger. In her arms, clutched to her breast, she holds a bouquet of mountain-ash, misty green touched here and there with red.

"Oh, thank you," I say, "thank you."

That wasn't the word.

It's dark. I kiss her.

A still life magically takes form in my mind.

She poses for me, a nude rounded figure.

I approach her timidly. I confess it was the first time I had seen a nude.

Though she was almost my fiancée, I was nevertheless afraid to go near her, to get any closer, to touch all that loveliness.

As if a feast were spread before your eyes.

I made a study of it and hung it on the wall.

The next day my mother comes into my room and sees that study.

"What's that?"

A naked woman, breasts, dark spots.

I'm embarrassed; so is she.

"Take that girl away!" she says.

"Dear little Mama! I love you very much. But . . . haven't you ever seen yourself in the nude? As for me, I only look and sketch her. That's all."

However I obeyed my mother. I put away the canvas and, in place of that nude, I painted another picture, a procession.

Soon, I moved into another room, in a policeman's house.

I was very pleased with it. It seemed to me he watched over me day and night.

You can paint whatever you wish.

Bella can come and go at will.

The policeman was tall, with a drooping mustache—just like the pictures.

Opposite his house was the Ilynsky church. It was snowing.

One night, as I was going out with Bella to take her

back to her parents' house, while we were kissing each other our feet struck against a large bundle.

"What's that?"

A baby—abandoned. A frail little piece of flesh, swathed in dark wool. It was whimpering.

Proudly I hand it over to my big policeman.

Another time it is night, Bella cannot get out: the door is locked.

The little lamp is smoking. In front of the kitchen stove, fire irons are resting. Everything is motionless. A few empty casseroles lie about.

How shall I get her out? What will the neighbors think?

"Look," I tell her, "crawl through the window."

That makes us laugh. I let her down out of the window into the alley.

The next day people whispered in the courtyard and on the street: "You know, she even climbs through the window to get into his room and to get out. It's gone that far!"

Try and tell them my fiancée is purer than Raphael's Madonna and I'm an angel!

Rooms, alcoves to rent, as many as you wish. Advertisements were as plentiful as the dampness. On my arrival in Petersburg, I had rented a room that I shared with a young sculptor just beginning his career, whom the writer Sholem Aleichem considered a future Antokolsky —he was soon to become a doctor.

He roared like a wild animal and hurled himself furiously on his clay to keep it from drying out.

Is that any of my business?

All the same I'm a man. I can't wake up every time he sniffs.

One day I threw the lamp at his head.

"Get out," I told him, "Go to your Sholem Aleichem: I want to be alone."

Immediately after I arrived in the capital, I went to take the examination for admission to Baron Stieglitz's School of Arts and Crafts.

This, I thought, as I looked at the building, is where one obtains permission to live in the capital and a subsidy on which to live.

But the studies, copying those long plaster decorative designs that looked to me like things in a department store, all alarmed me.

I thought: those designs have been chosen on purpose to frighten, to embarrass the Jewish pupils and keep them from getting the authorization they need.

Alas! My presentiment was correct.

I failed the examination. I received neither recommendation nor subsidy. Nothing was to be done about it!

I was obliged to enroll in an easier school, the one conducted by the Society for the Protection of the Arts, where I entered the third year without an examination.

What did I do there? I wouldn't know what to say.

Numerous plaster heads of Greek and Roman citizens projected from every corner and I, poor country lad, was obliged to acquaint myself thoroughly with the wretched nostrils of Alexander of Macedonia or some other plaster imbecile.

Sometimes I walked up to those noses and punched

them. And, from the back of the room, I gazed a long time at Venus's dusty breasts.

Though my style of painting was commended, I saw no results.

I couldn't look dispassionately on those cab driver-pupils who dug their erasers into their paper and sweated as if they were using a shovel.

At heart they weren't bad fellows. My Semitic appearance aroused their curiosity. They even advised me to collect all my sketches (I haven't kept a single one) and enter them in the competition.

When I found I was one of four chosen for a scholarship, I thought I had put the past behind me forever. For one year I received ten roubles a month. I was rich and I treated myself almost daily to a meal in a little restaurant on Zoukowskaja Street—after which, as a rule, I nearly passed out.

The sculptor Guinzbourg came to my rescue. Short, skinny, a long black goatee, an excellent man. I remember him with particular gratitude.

His studio in the Academy of Fine Arts, crammed with souvenirs of his master, Antokolsky, and his own busts of contemporary celebrities, seemed to me a center inhabited by the elect who had traveled life's hard road.

As a matter of fact, that little man knew intimately Leo Tolstoy, Stassoff, Repin, Gorky, Chaliapin, and many others. He was at the height of his fame, whereas I—I was nothing at all, without the right to live, without the most modest monthly income.

I don't know whether he found any particular merit in my adolescent studies.

However, he provided me, as was his habit, with a letter of recommendation to Baron David Guinzbourg. The latter, who saw a future Antokolsky in every boy presented to him, assigned me a monthly subsidy of ten roubles, to be paid for several months only.

And after that, you're on your own!

That erudite Baron, an intimate friend of Stassoff, knew next to nothing about art. But he thought it his duty to converse graciously with me, telling me stories with a moral to prove that artists must learn to be prudent.

"There's the wife of Antokolsky, for example. She was no good. It seems she drove beggars from her door. Look out for that! Be prudent! . . . A wife can be of great importance in an artist's life."

I listened respectfully—and thought of something else.

I drew his subsidy for four or five months.

And I thought: the Baron receives me nicely enough; he talks with me. Why then can he not subsidize all my needs so that I can live and work?

One day when I went to collect the ten roubles, his imposing manservant told me, as he held out the money:

"Here they are and it's the last time."

Had the Baron and his family given a thought to what was to become of me when I left his magnificent staircase? Could I, at seventeen, earn a living with my sketches? Or did he simply think: Look our for yourself, sell newspapers.

Then why had he done me the favor of talking with me as though he had faith in my artistic ability?

81   I couldn't understand. And there was nothing to understand.

I was the one who suffered, no one else. I hadn't even a nook where I could draw.

Good-bye, Baron!

At that time I was introduced to a group of prominent art patrons. Everywhere, in their drawing rooms, I felt as if I'd just come out of the bath, my face red and overheated.

Oh! for permission to live in the capital!

Here I am, a servant in the house of lawyer Goldberg!

Lawyers have the right to keep Jewish servants.

But, according to the law, I must live in his house and take my meals there. We became great friends.

In the spring he took me to their property of Narwa where, in the vast drawing room, in the shade of the trees and on the seashore, his wife and her sisters, the Germontes, radiated so much affection.

Dear Goldberg! I see you before me now.

But before I met those Maecenases I didn't know where to lay my head.

My means did not permit me to rent a room; I was forced to content myself with nooks and alcoves. I didn't even have a bed to myself. I had to share it with a workingman. It's true, he was an angel, that workingman with the very black mustache.

He was so kind to me he even flattened himself against the wall to give me more room. Turning my back on him and my face to the window, I breathed in the fresh air.

In those communal recesses, with laborers and pushcart vendors for neighbors, there was nothing for me to do but stretch out on the edge of my bed and think about myself. What else? And dreams overwhelmed me: a bedroom, square, empty. In one corner, a single bed and me on it. It is getting dark.

Suddenly, the ceiling opens and a winged creature descends with great commotion, filling the room with movement and clouds.

A swish of wings fluttering.

I think: an angel! I can't open my eyes; it's too bright, too luminous.

After rummaging about on all sides, he rises and passes through the opening in the ceiling, carrying with him all the light and the blue air.

Once again it is dark. I wake up.

My picture "The Apparition" evokes that dream.

Another time I rented half a room, somewhere on Panteleïmonowsky Street. At night I could not understand where all the noise, that kept me from sleeping, came from. The other half of the room was separated from mine only by a curtain. Why those snores?

Another time, the tenant of the other half of the room, a drunkard, a typographer by day and by night an accordion player in the amusement park, came home late at night and, after having stuffed himself with raw cabbage, insisted upon making love to his wife.

She pushed him away, took refuge in my half of the room and then fled into the passage, clad only in her nightgown. He pursued her, knife in hand.

"How dare you refuse yourself to me, your lawful husband?"

I realized then that, in Russia, Jews are not the only

ones who have no right to live, but also many Russians, crowded together like lice in one's hair. My God!

I moved again.

My roommate was a Persian of rather mysterious background. He had fled his country, where he had been at one time a revolutionary, at another, attached to the suite of the former Shah. Not much was known about him.

He liked me, the way one likes a bird, while he dreamed of his Persia and of his mysterious affairs.

Later, I learned that this former follower of the Shah had committed suicide on the boulevards in Paris.

However, my torments were renewed for lack of that famous permit and also because the time for my military service was drawing near.

One day, returning to Petersburg after the holidays, without a pass, I was arrested by the Commissioner in person.

As he was the dispenser of passports and had not received the tip he'd hoped for (I hadn't understood), he insulted me violently and ordered:

"Hey, there! Arrest him. . . . he entered the capital without permission! Put him into the lockup with the thieves, for now. Later you can send him to prison."

And this was done.

Thank God! At last I have peace.

Here, at least, I have the right to live. Here I'll be at rest, eat my fill and perhaps I'll even be able to draw in peace?

Nowhere else had I felt so relaxed as in that cell

where they took off all my clothes and made me put on the prison uniform.

The slang of thieves and prostitutes was very amusing. They neither cursed me nor shoved me around. I even had their respect.

Later I was transferred to a separate cell with a fantastic old man.

I took pleasure in rushing into that lavatory time and again—without any need—in deciphering the scribbles that covered walls and doors, in lingering before a bowl of water at the long table in the dining hall.

And in that cell for two, when the electricity went off, as it always did towards nine o'clock at night, so that we could neither read, nor draw, I slept soundly. I even began to dream again.

Here is one of those dreams: Several children of the same father—I'm one of them—are somewhere at the seashore.

All, except me, are shut up in a high, wide lion's cage. The father, an orangoutang, with a tawny muzzle, holds a whip in his hand, alternately threatening us and groaning.

All of a sudden, we are seized with a desire to go in bathing, like my older brother Wrubel, the Russian painter, who was also there, I don't know why, among my numerous brothers.

The first one they brought out was Wrubel.

I remember seeing him, our well-beloved, take off his clothes. In the distance we see his golden legs open like scissors. He swims towards the open sea. But the wild sea roars, boils up. An onrush of angry swells pile up into high crests. The waves, heavy as molasses, thunder deafeningly. What has become of my poor brother? We are all worried. All one can see, afar off, is his little head—no more gleaming legs.

At last, even his head disappears.

One arm is thrust out of the water, and then nothing more.

All the children yelled:

"He's drowned; our eldest brother, Wrubel, is drowned . . ."

The father repeated in his deep voice: "He's drowned, our son, Wrubel. All we have left is a painter son, you, my son."

That was me.

I woke up,

Freed at last from jail, I decided to train myself in some sort of profession that would allow me to have a permit to live in the capital. I therefore became an apprentice to a sign painter in order to get a certificate from a professional school.

I dreaded the examination. Perhaps I could draw fruit or a Turk smoking, but I'd surely come to grief on the letters. However, I took a passionate interest in those signs and I did a whole series of them.

I liked to see my signs swinging in the market place above the entrance to a butcher shop or a fruit shop, and near them a pig or a chicken tenderly scratching itself, while wind and rain, unconcerned, splashed them with mud.

11

But it was useless for me to follow the courses at the School for the Protection of the Arts. I knew I would never be satisfied with it.

The teaching was non-existent. Our director, Roehrich, wrote unreadable poems and books on history and archaeology and, smiling, teeth clenched, he would read fragments of them—I don't know why—even to me, a pupil in his school, as if I understood a word of it.

I wasted two years in that school. It was cold in the classrooms. To the smell of dampness was added that of clay, paints, pickled cabbage and stagnant water in the Moyky Canal, so many odors, real or imaginary.

Though I forced myself to work, I had only a feeling of bitterness. And yet, around me I heard nothing but praise. I realized there was no sense in going on this way.

From time to time my long-legged professor in the still-life class reprimanded me before the whole room.

It's true, his pupils' miserable daubs particularly infuriated me.

Students spent several years in the same class.

I didn't know what to do, nor how. Smear the paper with charcoal and fingers or yawn like the others.

To my professor my sketches were meaningless daubs.

After hearing criticisms like: "What asininity have you drawn there?" and, "a scholarship student, eh!" I left the school forever.

At that period Bakst's school in Petersburg was begining to be famous.

As far removed from the Academy as from the School for the Protection of the Arts, it was the only school animated by a breath from Europe. But the thirty roubles monthly frightened me. Where would I get them?

M. Sew, who always told me, smiling: "The drawing, above all, the drawing! Think of that!" gave me a letter of recommendation to M. Bakst.

Taking my courage in both hands, I collected my sketches, those done in class and others painted at home, and carried them to Bakst's residence on Serguiewskaia Street.

"The master is still asleep," Leon Bakst's mysterious maid told me.

One o'clock in the afternoon and still in bed, I thought.

Silence. No shouts of children, no perfume of a woman. On the walls, paintings of Greek gods, a black velvet altar-curtain, from a synagogue, embroidered in silver. Strange! As once before I stammered to M. Penne: "My name is Marc. I've a very sensitive stomach and no money, but people say I have talent," so I whisper timidly in Bakst's anteroom.

He's still asleep, but he'll come soon. I must think about what I'm going to say to him.

That's it! I'll be sure to tell him, I just know it: "My father is a simple clerk and your apartment is very clean . . ."

I had never been so upset by waiting.

At last, here he is. I've never forgotten the smile, tinged with pity, or maybe kindness, with which he welcomed me.

It seemed to me mere chance that he was wearing European clothes. He is a Jew. Above his ears reddish locks curled. He could have been my uncle, my brother.

I had just remembered that he was born not far from my ghetto and that he, too, had been a pink-and-white youngster like me: perhaps he even stammered the way I did.

To enter Bakst's school, to see him, upset me, I don't know why.

Bakst. Europe. Paris.

He'll understand me; he'll understand why I stammer, why I'm pale, why I'm so often sad and even why I paint with lilac colors.

He stood before me, smiling slightly and showing a row of shining teeth, pink and golden.

"What can I do for you?" he said.

On his lips, certain words drawled strangely, a special accent that made him appear more European than ever.

His fame, after the Russian season abroad, turned my head, I don't know why.

"Let me see your studies," he said to me.

I . . . oh, well! . . . No chance now to draw back or to be timid. If my first visit to Penne was important only to my mother, the one I was making to Bakst was tremendously important to me, and his opinion (whatever it might be) decisive.

I wanted only one thing: that there should be no mistake.

Would he consider that I had talent, yes or no?

As he turned my sketches over which, one by one, I picked up from the floor where I had piled them up, he said, drawling out the words in his lordly accent:

"Ye . . . es . . . es . . . es! There's talent here; but

89   you've been sp-oi-led, you're on the wrong track . . . sp-oi-l-ed."

Enough! My God, me? The scholarship pupil of the School for the Protection of the Arts, the one on whom the director mechanically lavished his beaming smiles, the student whose style (curse it!) was praised, but who, constantly doubting himself, took no satisfaction in his own daubings.

However Bakst's voice, his words—spoiled, but not completely—saved me.

Had anyone else spoken those words, I would have paid no attention. But Bakst's authority was too great for me to disregard his opinion. I heard it, standing, deeply moved, believing every word while, embarrassed, I rolled up my canvases and my sketches.

Never shall I forget that meeting with Bakst.

What is the use of pretending: something in his art would always be alien to me.

The fault lay perhaps not in him, but in the artistic society "Mir Iskoustva" of which he was a member and where stylization, aestheticism, all sorts of worldly manners and mannerisms flourished; for that society, the revolutionaries of contemporary art—Cézanne, Manet, Monet, Matisse and others—were merely initiators of a passing vogue.

Was it not the same with the celebrated Russian critic, Stassoff, who, dazzled, blinded by his national and ethnological prophecies then so much in vogue, led astray any number of contemporary artists? I, who didn't even know there was a Paris in the world, found in Bakst's school a Europe in miniature.

Bakst's pupils, all more or less gifted, at least knew where they were going. More and more I was convinced that I must forget everything I had learned.

I began to work. A model was posing, huge pink legs, blue background.

In the atelier, among the pupils, Countess Tolstoy, the dancer Nijinsky.

I'm intimidated again.

I had heard that Nijinsky was already a famous dancer and that he had been dismissed from the Imperial Theatre solely because of his brazen costumes.

His easel stood next to mine. He drew rather awkwardly, like a child.

When Bakst came up to him, he merely smiled and clapped Nijinsky lightly on the shoulder.

Nijinsky smiled at me too, as though he wanted to encourage in me a boldness of which I was not yet aware. That brought us closer together.

The study is finished. Bakst criticizes on Fridays.

He comes only once a week. Then all the pupils stop work. The easels are lined up. We are waiting for him. Here he is.

He goes from one canvas to the next, not knowing exactly to whom each belongs.

Not till afterwards does he ask: "Whose is this?" He says little—one or two words—but hypnosis, fright and the breath of Europe do the rest.

He is coming towards me. I'm lost. He speaks to me; or, more precisely, he speaks about my study though he doesn't know (or pretends not to know) that it's mine. He says a few casual words to me, the way one makes polite conversation.

All the pupils look at me pityingly.

"Whose sketch is this?" he asks at last.

"Mine."

"I thought so. Of course," he adds.

In an instant the memory of all my alcoves, all my dingy rooms, passes through my mind, but nowhere had I been as unhappy as after that remark of Bakst's.

I felt that things couldn't go on that way any longer. I made another study. Friday. Bakst arrives. No praise.

I fled from the atelier. For three months, Allia Bersen, who was sensitive and kind to me, paid uselessly for the lessons, while I was absent.

It was more than I could handle. The truth is, I'm incapable of learning. Or rather it's impossible to teach me. It's not without good reason that I was a bad pupil back in the days of the elementary school. I get nothing except by instinct. You understand? And academic theory has no hold on me.

In short, going to school was for me more a means of getting information, of communication, than of instruction proper.

After the disaster of my first two studies in Bakst's school—I did not understand the reason for that failure —I fled in order to orient myself and to make an effort to shake off the yoke that hindered me.

I didn't go back to school till three months later, for I was firmly decided not to give up but to win the master's approval in front of all those distinguished pupils.

I forgot all I had learned before and I made a new study.

The following Friday it was judged by Bakst and, as a mark of honor, hung on the studio wall.

It was not long before I realized that I had nothing more to learn in that school. All the more so as Bakst himself, following the Russian season abroad, left the school and Petersburg, forever.

I say, stammering:

"Leon Samuelevitch, could one . . . ? You know, Leon Samuelevitch, I'd like...to...to...go...to Paris."

"Ah! . . . If you wish. Tell me, do you know how to paint scenery?"

"Perfectly." (I hadn't the remotest idea!)

"Then, here are one hundred francs. Learn that profession well and I'll take you there."

But our paths separated and I left for Paris by myself . . .

I urged my father to rebel.

"Father," I said to him, "listen; you have a big son now, a painter. When will you get tired of enriching your boss with that infernal work of yours? Didn't I faint enough times in Petersburg? Haven't I eaten enough minced cutlets? What will become of me in Paris?"

And he, answering me:

"What, me go away? And you're the one who's going to feed me? I can just see that!"

Mama plucked up courage.

"My son, we are your parents. Write to us more often. Ask us for anything you need."

Beneath my feet, mother earth slipped away. The harsh river flowed turbulently; it wasn't the one beside which I embraced you . . .

The Ouspene church, on top of the hill, the dome

above it. The Dvina grows smaller and smaller in the distance. I'm not a youngster any more.

As soon as I learned how to express myself in Russian, I began to write poetry. As naturally as breathing.

What difference if it's a word or a sigh? I used to read my poetry to my friends. They too wrote poems, but as soon as I read them mine, theirs disappeared.

I suspected my friend V. . . . of passing off translations of foreign poems as his own creations.

I longed to show my verses to a real poet, one of those who get their poetry published.

I ventured to ask the sculptor, Guinzbourg, to submit them to one of his friends, a poet who at that time enjoyed a certain vogue.

But no sooner had I mentioned my desire (and how painful it was even to open my mouth), he began to pace about his studio, pushing his way between his statues and shouting:

"What? How's that? What's the use? A painter doesn't need that. It mustn't be allowed!"

I was startled, but at the same time, calmed.

"It's true, there is no necessity.

When, later, I met Alexander Blok, a poet of rare and subtle excellence, I again had a desire to show him my verses and get his opinion.

But before his eyes and his face I drew back as before a vision of life.

And I threw away, abandoned or lost, the one copybook that contained my juvenile poems.

Everyone is at home. In Petrograd the Duma is sitting. The *Retz* newspaper. The atmosphere is electric.

And I, I am painting my pictures. Mama supervises my painting. She thinks, for instance, that, in the picture "Birth," I should bandage the stomach of the woman in child-bed.

I immediately satisfy her desire.

That was right! The body takes on life!

Bella brings me some blue flowers, mixed with green leaves. She is all in white, with black gloves. I'm painting her portrait.

Once I've counted all the hedgerows in town, I paint "Death."

Once I've taken the pulse of all my family and friends, I paint "Marriage."

But I felt that if I stayed much longer in Vitebsk, I would be covered with hair and moss.

I roamed about the streets, I searched and prayed:

"God, Thou who hidest in the clouds or behind the shoemaker's house, grant that my soul may be revealed, the sorrowful soul of a stammering boy. Show me my way. I do not want to be like all the others; I want to see a new world."

As if in reply, the town seems to snap apart, like the strings of a violin, and all the inhabitants, leaving their usual places, begin to walk above the earth. People I know well, settle down on roofs and rest there.

All the colors turn upside down, dissolve into wine and my canvases gush it forth.

I am happy with all of you. But . . . have you ever heard of traditions, of Aix, of the painter with his ear cut off, of cubes, of squares, of Paris?

95   Vitebsk, I'm deserting you.
Stay alone with your herring!

I confess, I couldn't say that Paris attracted me greatly.

Nor did I have any enthusiasm when I left Vitebsk for Petersburg either. It was hard for me to define exactly what I wanted.

Too provincial, if I must admit it frankly.

Liking change and travel, I nevertheless dreamed only of being alone in a cage.

I often used to say that a little room, with a grating in the door through which someone could pass me my food, would have satisfied me forever.

Such are the feelings with which I went to Petersburg and later to Paris. But for the latter journey, I lacked the money.

If I were not to be lost among the thirty thousand artists who had come to Paris from every land and every nation, I must, first of all, be assured of the means to live there and to work.

At that time I was introduced to M. Vinaver, an eminent member of the Duma.

Do not imagine that only persons prominent in political or social circles could approach him!

With deep sorrow, I can say today that in him I lost a man who was very close to me, almost a father.

I remember his sparkling eyes, his eyebrows that moved slowly up and down, the sensitive cut of his mouth, his light brown beard, all that noble profile which I— always so diffident, alas!—did not dare to paint.

In spite of the difference between him and my father,

who never went anywhere but to the synagogue whereas M. Vinaver was elected by the people, they nevertheless had something in common. My father put me into the world and Vinaver made a painter of me.

Without him, I would perhaps have remained a photographer, would have settled in Vitebsk and would never have had any idea of Paris.

In my stay in Petersburg, I had neither permission to live there, nor the tiniest nook in which to live: no bed, no money.

More than once, I looked enviously at the kerosene lamp burning on the table.

See how comfortably it burns, I thought. It drinks its fill of oil and I . . . ?

I can scarcely sit on the chair, on the edge of the chair. And the chair doesn't belong to me. The chair without a room.

I don't even dare to sit down quietly. I'm hungry. I dream of the package of sausages received by a classmate of mine.

In general, I've been seeing bread and sausages in my dreams for years.

And, added to all that, a yearning to paint . . .

Somewhere down there, waiting for me, are green rabbis, peasants in their baths, red Jews, kind, intelligent, their staffs, their sacks, on the streets, in houses and even on roofs.

They wait for me, I wait for them, we wait for each other.

But, on the other hand, on the streets police are on

guard at the police station, porters in front of their doors, the "passportists" at the commissariat.

As I wandered along the streets, I read the menus at the doors of restaurants—like poems, "Today's Specialties," and the price of each dish.

Then it was that Vinaver put me up not far from his house, Zacharjewskaja Street, in the flat occupied by the editorial board of the magazine *Dawn.*

I copied a Levitan painting he owned. I liked it for its moonlight. As though candles shone behind the canvas.

I didn't dare to have that picture taken down from the wall where it had been hung, very high up, so I copied it standing on a chair.

I took that copy to a picture-framer who also made some enlargements.

To my great surprise, he paid me ten roubles.

Several days later as I passed his shop, I noticed my copy, prominently displayed in the window and bearing the signature "Levitan." The proprietor smiled at me amiably and asked me to make others for him.

A little later I took him a pile of my own canvases. Perhaps, I thought, he'll sell some of them.

But the next day, when I went to ask if he had sold anything, he looked surprised: "Pardon me, sir," he said, "but who are you? I don't know you."

That is the way I lost some fifty of my canvases.

Vinaver did everything he could to encourage me.

With M. Syrkine and M. Sew, he dreamt of seeing me become a second Antokolsky.

Every day, as he climbed the steps of his apartment, he would smile at me and ask:

"Well, how are you getting on?"

The editorial room was full of my canvases and sketches. It didn't look like an editorial room now, more like a studio. My thoughts on art mingled with the voices of the editors who came to discuss and work.

In the intervals and at the end of the meeting, they would walk through my "studio" and I would hide behind piled-up copies of "Dawn" that lined half of the room.

Vinaver was the first person in my life to buy two pictures from me.

Lawyer and famous member of Parliament that he was, he nevertheless liked those poor Jews who come down with the bride, the bridegroom and the musicians from the top of my canvas.

One day, panting, breathless, he runs into the editorial studio and tells me:

"Quick! Get together your best canvases and come up to my apartment. A collector saw your pictures at my house; he's keenly interested in them."

Excited and dismayed at seeing Vinaver himself come to my room, I couldn't find anything good.

Once, at Passover, Vinaver invited me to his house for dinner.

The reflection of the blazing candles, their odor mingling with the dark ochre of Vinaver's complexion, glowed in the room.

His wife, giving orders smilingly, looked as though she had stepped out of a fresco by Veronese.

The table shone in anticipation of the prophet Elijah.

99   Later, Vinaver came to see me many times and, smiling, would ask: "Well, how are things going?"

I dared not show him my pictures for fear he would not like them. He often used to say he was a rank outsider in matters of art.

But the outsiders are the critics I like best.

In 1910, after he had selected two pictures, Vinaver guaranteed me a monthly subsidy that would permit me to live in Paris.

I set out.

Four days later, I arrived in Paris.

12

Only the great distance that separates Paris from my native town prevented me from returning to it immediately or at least after a week, or a month.

I even wanted to invent some sort of holiday as an excuse to go home.

The Louvre put an end to all those hesitations.

When I made the tour of the Veronese room and the rooms in which Manet, Delacroix, Courbet are hung, I wanted nothing more.

In my imagination Russia appeared like a paper balloon suspended from a parachute. The flattened pear of the balloon hung, cooled off, and slowly collapsed in the course of the years.

That's how Russian art appeared to me, or something like it.

Indeed, every time I happened to think of Russian art or to speak of it, I experienced the same troubled and confused emotions, full of bitterness and resentment.

It was as though Russian art had been inevitably doomed to follow along in the wake of the West.

If Russian painters were doomed to be pupils of the West, they were, I thought, rather faithless pupils, and by their very nature. The best Russian realist shocks the realism of Courbet.

The most genuine Russian impressionism leaves one perplexed when you compare it with Monet and Pissarro.

Here, in the Louvre, before the canvases of Manet, Millet and others, I understood why I could not ally myself with Russia and Russian art. Why my very speech is foreign to them.

101   Why they do not trust me. Why artists' circles ignored me.

Why, in Russia, I am only the fifth wheel.

And why everything I do seems eccentric to them and everything they do seems superfluous to me. But why?

I cannot talk about it any more.

I love Russia.

In Paris I thought I had found everything, in particular the art of my craft.

Everywhere I saw convincing proof of it in the museums and in the Salons.

Perhaps the East had lost its way in my soul; or the memory of that dog-bite re-echoed in my mind.

But it was not only in my profession that I sought the meaning of art.

It was as though the gods stood before me.

I didn't want to think any more about the neo-classicism of David, of Ingres, the romanticism of Delacroix and the reconstruction of early drawings of the followers of Cézanne and of Cubism.

I felt we were still playing around on the surface, that we are afraid of plunging into chaos, of shattering, of turning upside down the familiar ground under our feet.

The day after my arrival, I went to the Salon des Indépendants.

The friend who went with me had warned me it would be impossible to cover the entire Salon in a single day. He, for example, came out exhausted every time he visited it. Pitying him from the bottom of my heart but following my own method, I rushed through all the first rooms as if I were racing ahead of a torrent and I dashed towards the middle rooms.

That's the way I conserved my strength.

I went straight to the heart of French painting of 1910.

And there I clung.

No academy could have given me all I discovered by gorging myself on the exhibitions of Paris, on its picture shop windows, its museums.

Beginning with the Markets where, for lack of money, I bought only a piece of a long cucumber, the working-man in his blue overalls, the most zealous followers of Cubism, everything showed a definite feeling for order, clarity, an accurate sense of form, of a more painterly type of painting even in the works of lesser artists.

I don't know whether anyone has been able to form a clearer idea than I of the almost insurmountable difference which, up to 1914, separated French painting from the painting of other lands. It seems to me they had very little notion of it abroad.

As for me, I've never stopped thinking about that.

It is not a question of the natural aptitudes, more or less great, of an individual or of a people.

Other forces come into play, organic or psycho-physical on the whole, that predispose one either to music, painting, literature, or sleep.

After living for some time in a studio at the Impasse du Maine, I moved into another studio more in keeping with my means, "La Ruche" (The Beehive).

That was the name given to a hundred or so studios surrounded by a little garden and very close to the

Vaugirard slaughterhouses. In those studios lived the artistic Bohemia of every land.

While in the Russian ateliers an offended model sobbed; from the Italians' came the sound of songs and the twanging of a guitar, and from the Jews debates and arguments, I sat alone in my studio before my kerosene lamp. A studio jammed with pictures, with canvases which, moreover, were not really canvases but my table napkins, my bed sheets, my nightshirts torn into pieces.

Two or three o'clock in the morning. The sky is blue. Dawn is breaking. Down below and a little way off, they are slaughtering cattle, the cows low and I paint them.

I used to stay up all night long. It's now a week since the studio has been cleaned. Frames, eggshells, empty soup cans lie around helter-skelter.

My lamp burned, and I with it.

It burned until its glare hardened in the blue of morning.

Not until then did I climb up into my garret. I should have gone down into the street and bought some hot croissants on tick, but I went to bed. Later the cleaning woman came; I wasn't sure whether she came to set the studio to rights (is that absolutely necessary? At least, don't touch my table!) or whether she wanted to come up and be with me.

On the shelves, reproductions of El Greco, of Cézanne, lay side by side with the remnants of a herring I had cut in two, the head for the first day, the tail for the next and, thank God, a few crusts of bread.

But perhaps Cendrars will come and take me out to lunch.

Before my friends entered the studio, they always had to wait. That was to give me time to tidy up, to put on my clothes, for I worked in the nude. In general, I can't stand clothes, I'd rather not wear them and I have no taste in dressing.

No one buys my pictures.

I didn't think that was possible.

Once only, M. Malpel offered me twenty-five francs for a picture I was showing in the Salon—in case I shouldn't sell it.

"But, by all means, why wait!"

I don't know now what happened; twenty years later the pictures are selling. They even say that a real Frenchman, Gustave Coquiot, collects my pictures.

I should go to see him and thank him.

And I, on the eve of war, scattered haphazard nearly four hundred of my canvases in Germany, Holland, Paris, a bit everywhere.

No matter. At least, since they cost them nothing, the people who have them will take the trouble to hang them on their walls.

Once in Paris, I went to the Diaghileff ballet to see Bakst and Nijinsky. All his life long, Diaghileff has never known whether to speak to me or how.

For me, his ballets had the same objective as the "Mir Iskoustva" which, furthermore, was also founded by Diaghileff. All the discoveries, the lucky finds, the "novelties" were filtered through it, polished to reach society in a piquant and sophisticated style.

As for me, I'm the son of workers and often, in a

drawing room, for want of something to do, I feel inclined to dirty the shining floors.

The moment I pushed open the door leading backstage, I saw Bakst in the distance.

Something red-haired and pink smiled at me benevolently.

Nijinsky comes running up, grabs me by the shoulders. But the next moment he's running towards the stage where Karsavina is waiting for him; they were giving the "Spectre of the Rose."

With a fatherly gesture, Bakst stops him.

"Wazia, wait, come here," And he arranges his wide scarf for him.

Near him, d'Anunzio, small, with a thin mustache, is flirting tenderly with Ida Rubenstein.

"So you came, after all?" Bakst flings at me abruptly.

I'm embarrassed. However, he had advised me not to go to Paris, warning me that I ran the risk of dying of hunger there and that I was not to count on him.

At that time he was still in Petersburg and he had given me a hundred francs in the hope that I would become his assistant decorator. But, when he saw how awkward I was at scene-painting, he chucked me.

In spite of his warning I left Petersburg and here I am in front of him. I find it difficult to talk to him. I know that Bakst is extremely nervous. So am I. I'm not offended. But after all! Was I to stay in Russia?

Back there, still a boy, at every step I felt—or rather, people made me feel!—that I was a Jew.

When I had to deal with the young artists' group,

they hung my pictures—if they consented to hang them at all—in the farthest, and darkest, corner.

When, on Bakst's advice, I sent a few canvases to the "Mir Iskoustva" exhibition, they were calmly left behind in the apartment of one of the members, whereas almost every Russian painter of any standing whatever, was invited to become a member of the society.

And I thought: surely it's because I'm a Jew and I have no country.

Paris! No word sounded sweeter to me!

To tell the truth, at that moment, it made little difference to me whether Bakst came to see me or not.

But it was he who, on bidding me good-bye, said:

"I'll stop by your place and see what you're doing."

One day he came.

"Now," he said, "your colors sing."

Those were the last words addressed by Professor Bakst to his ex-pupil.

What he saw perhaps convinced him that I had left my ghetto behind and that here, in "La Ruche," in Paris, in France, in Europe, I am a man.

More than once in my search for art, I wandered through the rue Laffitte, gazing at the hundreds of Renoirs, Pissarros, Monets at Durand-Ruel's.

I was particularly drawn to Vollard's shop. But I didn't dare go in.

In the dark, dusty shop windows, nothing but old newspapers and a little statue by Maillol, as if it had wandered there by mistake. My eyes searched eagerly for the Cézannes.

They are on the wall at the back, unframed. I press

against the glass, flattening my nose, and suddenly I come upon Vollard himself.

He is alone in the middle of the shop and he is wearing an overcoat.

I hesitate to go in. He looks bad-tempered. I don't dare.

But at Bernheim's, Place de la Madeleine, the show windows are lighted up as if for a wedding.

There are Van Gogh, Gauguin, Matisse.

Look around, come in and go out, as you please!

That is what I did once or twice a week.

But it was at the Louvre that I felt most at home.

Friends long vanished. Their prayers, mine. Their canvases light my childish face.

Rembrandt captivated me and more than once I stopped before Chardin, Fouquet, Géricault.

A friend from "La Ruche" painted some pictures and took them to the Market to sell.

One day I said to him:

"Perhaps I could sell something at the Market, too."

He painted women, in crinolines, walking in a park. That wasn't my style, but a landscape à la Corot, why not?

I took a photograph, but the more I tried to paint like Corot, the farther I got from it and I ended à la Chagall.

My friend made fun of me. You can imagine my surprise when I found that canvas later in the drawing room of an art collector.

With a letter from Canudo, in which he praised me far too lavishly, I went to M. Doucet to show him a folder of about fifty water colors. I had the vague hope that perhaps he would buy something.

After I'd waited a quarter of an hour in his anteroom, his servant came in and handed me my folder.

"We don't need the 'best colorist of our day,'" he said in the name of his employer.

Another letter of recommendation from Canudo to a cinema producer was more successful.

They were filming a movie in which a number of artists were to be shown. I was one of them. All of us were working in a professor's atelier. I don't recall whether the professor or one of his pupils was to fall in love with the model or perhaps with a customer.

From the atelier, the scene moved to a terrace overlooking the shores of a lake. On that terrace stood a large table, laden with food. We artists sat down around the table and ate with gusto, while they shot the scene. I ate all I could.

It was worse afterwards when they suggested that we take a sail in a boat, each gentleman with his lady.

My lady was a rather boring and not very photogenic girl. As I was the man, I was supposed to sail the boat—which I hadn't the faintest idea how to do.

Our boat is far from shore. The photographer turns and shouts at me: "Steer, for God's sake, steer!" Too bad, I'm not the right man for the job.

The young girl was furious. Nevertheless, when I appeared at the cashier's window, my costume under my arm, I was given a few francs for that day's work.

I'm sorry I never saw that film.

Later, someone told me he had seen me on the screen.

In those days, one-man exhibits were rare: Matisse and Bonnard were almost the only ones to have them. The idea never so much as entered our heads.

I frequented the ateliers and the academies of Montparnasse and at the same time I was eagerly preparing for the Salons.

But how could I carry such conspicuous canvases through "La Ruche" and across Paris?

A good-hearted refugee agreed to take care of it, more for laughs than for anything else.

On the way my handcart met other handcarts also carrying pictures to the Salon. All of them were heading towards the wooden booths near the Place de l'Alma.

There I was shortly to see what distinguished my work from traditional French painting.

At last, the pictures are hung. In an hour the vernissage. But the censor walks over to my canvases and orders one of them removed: "The Ass and the Woman."

My friend and I try to persuade him:

"But, sir, it's not at all what you think. No pornography is intended."

It's settled.

He agrees. The picture is hung again.

When I complained of being persecuted even in the Salon, the wife of a doctor whom I sometimes visited for conversation and consolation, told me:

"Well, all the better. That's what you deserve. Then don't paint that kind of picture."

I was only twenty, but I was already beginning to fear people.

But then the poet Rubiner came, Cendrars came and

the light in his eyes was enough to console me. Many a time he gave me advice, for he was anxious about me, but I never listened to him, though he was right.

He persuaded me that I could work peacefully side by side with proud cubists for whom I was perhaps a nobody.

They did not bother me. I looked at them out of the corner of my eye and I thought:

"Let them eat their fill of their square pears on their triangular tables!"

Undoubtedly my early trends were a little strange to the French. And I looked at them with so much love! It was painful.

But my art, I thought, is perhaps a wild art, a blazing quicksilver, a blue soul flashing on my canvases.

And I thought: Down with naturalism, impressionism and realistic cubism!

They make me sad and they cramp me.

All questions—volume, perspective, Cézanne, African sculpture—are brought on the carpet.

Where are we going? What is this era that sings hymns to technical art, that makes a god of formalism?

May our folly be welcomed!

An expiatory bath. A revolution of fundamentals, not only of the surface.

Don't call me temperamental! On the contrary, I'm a realist. I love the earth.

I tore myself away for a while from the courtyards of my native town and here I am, escaped into the circles and salons of French poets and painters.

111   There is Canudo. Black goatee, burning eyes.

Every Friday you can meet at his house Gleizes, Metz-inger, La Fresnaye, Léger, Raynal, Valentine de Sand-Point, accompanied by her three young admirers: Segonzac, professor at the academy "La Palette", where I have some-times worked; Lhote, Luc-Albert Moreau and so many, many others. It was warm and pleasant there.

Delaunay was particularly active. To me he was an enigma. At the Salon, I was impressed by the size of his canvases. He carried them triumphantly to the far end of the place, winking an eye as if to say: "Well, what about it?"

Canudo received me warmly and I shall never forget him. He took me here and there and one night, in his drawing room, he even arranged an exhibition of my sketches, spreading them out on tables, armchairs, all over the place.

Once, at the café, he said to me:

"Your head reminds me of Christ's." And grabbing a newspaper he flung it on the floor:

"To hell with it! There's nothing about me in it!"

With you I spring into the depths of Montjoie. As if dazzling lights flashed around you. As if a flight of white seagulls, or flakes of snowy spots, in single file, rose towards the sky.

There, another flame, light and clear-toned, Blaise, my friend Cendrars.

A chrome smock, socks each of a different color. Waves of sunshine, poverty and rhymes.

Threads of colors. Of liquid, flaming art.

Enthusiasm for pictures scarcely conceived. Heads, disjointed limbs, flying cows.

I remember all that, and you, Cendrars?

He was the first to come to see me at "La Ruche."

He read me his poems, looking out of the open window and into my eyes; he smiled at my canvases and both of us roared with laughter.

There was André Salmon. But where is he?

I hear his name spoken. His pale face glows. I have just shaken hands with him.

Here is Max Jacob. He looks like a Jew.

That's the way he looked to me alongside Apollinaire.

One day we went together to lunch not far from "La Ruche."

I wasn't sure whether he had even forty sous in his pocket. And he, did he think I had enough to pay for the meal?

We lunched on salad, sauce, salt, everything that begins with an "s."

Afterwards, we climbed slowly up to his place in Montmartre. He had much free time and I had even more.

At last, his apartment house, his courtyard, his dark little hole, the entrance door at the side—a regular Vitebsk courtyard. Little pictures are hung in the entrance, just beyond the threshold.

What did we talk about? In what language?

I understood very little. To tell the truth, I was alarmed.

His eyes glistened and rolled constantly. He stretched his body, moved about restlessly. Suddenly, he was quiet. Moving his half-opened mouth, he whistled. Then he laughed and his eyes, his chin, his arms, called to me, captivated me.

I said to myself: "If I follow him, he will devour me whole and throw my bones out of the window."

Here is the garret of Apollinaire, that gentle Zeus.

In verses, in numbers, in flowing syllables, he blazed a trail for all of us.

He came out of his corner bedroom and a smile spread slowly over his broad face. His nose was sharply pointed and his gentle, mysterious eyes sang of voluptuousness. He carried his stomach as if it were a collection of complete works and his legs gesticulated like arms.

In his garret there were always many discussions.

In one corner sits a nondescript little man.

Apollinaire goes over to him and wakes him:

"Do you know what we must do, Monsieur Walden? We must arrange an exhibit of this young man's works. You don't know him? . . . Monsieur Chagall . . ."

One day Apollinaire and I went out together to dine at Baty's in Montparnasse.

On the way, he suddenly stopped:

"Look, there's Degas. He's crossing the street. He's blind."

Alone, frowning, looking surly, Degas was striding along, leaning on his cane.

While we were eating, I asked Apollinaire why he didn't introduce me to Picasso.

"Picasso? Do you want to commit suicide? That's the way all his friends end," replied Apollinaire, smiling as always.

What a whale of an appetite, I thought, as I watched him eat.

Perhaps he has to eat so much to feed his mind.

Maybe you can eat talent. Eat, and above all, drink, and perhaps the rest will come of itself.

Wine rang in his glass, meat clattered between his teeth. And all the while he was greeting people right and left. Acquaintances on every side!

Oh! Oh! Oh! Ah! Ah! Ah!

And at the slightest pause, he emptied his glass, resplendent in his huge napkin.

Lunch over, swaying and licking our lips, we walked back to "La Ruche."

"You've never been here?"

"That's where Bohemians, Italians and Jews live; there are some young girls, too. Perhaps we'll find Cendrars in the corner café, Passage de Dantzig."

"We'll surprise him. He'll open his mouth as wide as two eggs, and quickly tuck in his pockets some verses he's just written."

I dare not show Apollinaire my canvases.

"I know, you're the standard bearer of Cubism. But I should like something else."

What else? I'm embarrassed.

We go down the dark corridor where water drips ceaselessly, where piles of garbage are heaped up.

A round landing; a dozen or so doors with numbers on them.

I open mine.

Apollinaire enters cautiously, as if he were afraid the

115 whole building might suddenly collapse and drag him down in the ruins.

Personally I do not think a scientific bent is a good thing for art.

Impressionism and Cubism are foreign to me.

Art seems to me to be above all a state of soul.

All souls are sacred, the soul of all the bipeds in every quarter of the globe.

Only the upright heart that has its own logic and its own reason is free.

The soul that has reached by itself that level which men call literature, the illogic, is the purest.

I am not speaking of the old realism, nor of the symbolism-romanticism that has contributed very little; nor of mythology either, nor of any sort of fantasy, but of what, my God?

You will say, those schools are merely formal trappings.

Primitive art already possessed the technical perfection towards which present generations strive, juggling and even falling into stylization.

I compared these formal trappings with the Pope of Rome, sumptuously garbed, compared to the naked Christ, or the ornate church, to prayer in the open fields.

Apollinaire sat down. He blushed, swelled out his chest, smiled and murmured: "Supernatural! . . ."

The next day I received a letter, a poem dedicated to me: "Rotsoge."

Like beating rain, the meaning of your words strikes us.

Surely you are dreaming today of aquarelles, of the

new surface of painting, of poets of ravaged destiny, of us all of whom in times past you spoke.

Has he gone, has he faded away or is he still with us, with his brilliant smile on his mortal face?

And I am dragging out my days on the Place de la Concorde or near the Luxembourg Gardens.

I look at Danton and Watteau, I pull off leaves.

Oh! If astride the stone chimera of Notre Dame I could manage with my arms and my legs to trace my way in the sky!

There it is! Paris, you are my second Vitebsk!

I often said: I'm not an artist. Well then, a cow, eh?

What does it matter? I've even thought of putting my picture on my visiting-card.

Apparently in those days, it was the cow that was directing world politics.

Cubism made mincemeat of her, expressionism twisted her.

And suddenly, in the East, those portents were materialized.

With my own eyes I saw the paintings of Derain, Juan Gris and others in the Kahnweiler Gallery crack and wrinkle. The paint kept falling off.

It seemed that I carried the first elements of that stormy period with me when I went to Berlin to see my exhibition.

In two little rooms of the editorial office of the review *Der Sturm,* my canvases, without frames, were hung close together; a hundred of my aquarelles were simply scattered around on tables.

My pictures swelled in the Potsdamerstrasse while, nearby, guns were being loaded.

Can we help it if we see world events only through canvas and painting materials, thickening and quivering like noxious gases?

Europe was going to war. Picasso, Cubism is done for.

Who cares about Serbia? Mow down all those barefoot peasants!

Set Russia afire and all of us with her . . .

As I was in Berlin, I didn't realize that, before a month was up, that bloody comedy would begin, as the result of which the whole world (and Chagall with it) would be transformed into a new stage on which tremendous mass-scale productions would be given.

No presentiment troubled me sufficiently to keep me from going to Russia.

I had wanted to go there for three months; I was eager to attend my sister's wedding, and to see Bella again.

That fourth and last romance had very nearly died of inanition during those four years I had lived abroad. At the end of my stay in Paris, all that was left was a pile of letters. One year more and everything might be over between us.

After a brief stay in Berlin, I set out for Russia.

And I had no sooner reached Vilna than I said to a Frenchwoman who sat in my compartment:

"Well, this is Russia! Just look at it!" All the more as the porter was about to disappear with my luggage.

The Czar had taken it into his head to visit Odessa

and was receiving delegations at the Vilna station. Impossible to get out.

I remembered how they had led us, as school children, near the town to greet the Czar, who had come to Vitebsk to review a number of regiments that were about to go to the front (the Russo-Japanese war).

We started out long before dawn.

Hosts of boys, excited and sleepy, met on the way, and headed in long lines towards fields covered with snow.

We were drawn up along the edge of the highroad.

And so, standing ankle-deep in snow, we waited hour after hour for the imperial convoy to arrive.

Fearing an attempted assassination, the authorities had halted the train in mid-field.

At last, far off in the distance, the Czar appeared, looking very pale and wearing the uniform of a private.

Each of us would have liked to see him closer to, but, herded together like sheep as we were, it was impossible for us to budge.

Suddenly, a little chap broke from the ranks of schoolboys and, holding a petition above his head, walked towards the Czar.

In a second, Nicholas was enveloped in a cloud of princes, ministers, generals, glittering in gala uniforms. Extremely tall, robust, white-haired or bald, chests covered with medals, stern or smiling, they followed the Czar on horseback and on foot.

A light snow was falling. From near and far came the sound of cheers from thousands of soldiers. The frozen air absorbed the national anthem, transforming it at times into plaintive notes. Military bands played continually in several different places.

Covered with snow, the Czar, saluting lightly, walked at the head of the Army.

One after the other the regiments filed past him and departed for the front.

"But how deadly this town is! And here we are held in this station," I said to my companion.

"Poor things, you especially . . ."

"Don't worry, I'll put you in the carriage and you'll get to Tzarskoye to your Senator's house where you're going to be the governess."

Was this already Russia?

I scarcely knew it at all.

What had I ever seen of it? Where are Novgorod, Rostov, Kiev?

Where are they?

For my part, I've seen only Petrograd, Moscow, the little village of Lyozno and Vitebsk. Vitebsk is a place like no other; a strange town, an unhappy town, a boring town.

A town full of young girls who, whether from lack of time or inclination, I did not even approach. Dozens, hundreds of synagogues, butcher shops, people in the streets.

Is that Russia?

It's only my town, mine, which I have rediscovered.

I come back to it with emotion.

In that period I painted my series of Vitebsk of 1914. I painted everything I saw. I painted at my window. I never went out on the street with my box of paints.

I was satisfied with a hedge, a signpost, a floor, a chair.

Imagine yourself seated at the table, in front the samovar, a humble old man leans back in his chair.

I look questioningly at him: "Who are you?"

"What! You don't know me? You've never heard of the preacher of Slouzk?"

"Then listen; in that case, please come to my house. I'll make . . ." What shall I say? . . . How explain to him? I'm afraid he'll get up and go away.

He came, sat down on a chair and promptly fell asleep.

Have you seen the old man in green that I painted? That's the one.

Another old man passes by our house. Gray hair, sullen expression. A sack on his back . . .

I wonder: Is it possible for him to open his mouth, even to beg for charity?

Indeed, he says nothing. He enters and stays discreetly near the door. There he stands for a long time. And if you give him anything, he goes out, as he came in, without a word.

"Listen," I say to him, "don't you want to rest a while. Sit down. Like this. You don't mind, do you? You'll have a rest. I'll give you twenty kopeks. Just put on my father's prayer clothes and sit down."

You've seen my painting of that old man at prayer? That's the one.

It was good to be able to work in peace. Sometimes a man posed for me who had a face so tragic and old, but at the same time angelic. But I couldn't hold out more than half an hour . . . He stank too much.

"That's all, sir, you may go."

You've seen my old man reading? That's the one.

I painted, I painted and finally, though I protested a bit, I found myself, one rainy night, standing under a wedding crown, of the most authentic sort, just as in my pictures. I was blessed according to the ritual, as was proper.

But a long comedy preceded that ceremony. Here it is.

The parents and all the numerous family of my . . . yes . . . yes . . . of my wife, were not pleased with my origin.

Why not? My father, a simple clerk. My grandfather . . .

And they? Just imagine, they owned three jewelry stores in our town. In their showcases, multicolored fires glittered and sparkled from rings, pins and bracelets. On every side clocks and alarm clocks rang the hour. Accustomed as I was to other interiors, this one seemed to me fabulous.

At their house, three times a week, they prepared enormous cakes, apple, cheese, poppy-seed, at the sight of which I would have fainted. And at breakfast, they served mounds of those cakes which everybody fell upon furiously, in a frenzy of gluttony. And at home, at our house, a simple meal like a still life à la Chardin.

Their father fed on grapes as mine did on onions; and fowl which, at our house, was sacrificed only once a year on the eve of The Atonement, was never absent from their table.

Her grandfather, a white-haired old man with a long beard, wanders about the apartment, hunts for Russian books, Russian passports, and whatever he finds he throws into the stove, burns it. He cannot stand having his grandsons attend Russian schools.

Useless, useless.

They must all go to the cheder, become rabbis!

He himself does nothing but pray all day long. And on the Day of Atonement, he is completely out of his head.

But he's already too old to fast.

The great rabbi himself has authorized him to take several drops of milk during the day of fasting.

My wife holds the spoon for him.

He is bathed in tears, his tears fall on his beard, in the milk.

He is in despair. The spoon, shaking, scarcely wets his lips on the day of fasting.

I have no strength left to talk about it. My head is in a whirl.

My fiancée's mother said to her daughter:

"It looks to me as though he even puts rouge on his cheeks. What sort of a husband will he make, that boy as pink-cheeked as a girl? He'll never know how to earn his living."

But what can they do if that's the way she likes him.

Impossible to convince her.

"You'll starve with him, my daughter; you'll starve for nothing."

"And besides, he's an artist. What does that mean?"

"And what will everybody say . . ."

Thus my fiancée's family argued about me and, morning and night, she brought to my studio sweet cakes from her house, broiled fish, boiled milk, all sorts of decorative materials, even some boards which I used for an easel.

I had only to open my bedroom window, and blue air, love and flowers entered with her.

Dressed all in white or all in black, she seemed to float over my canvases for a long time, guiding my art.

I never finish a picture or an engraving without asking for her "yes" or "no."

So what did I care about her parents, her brothers! May God protect them!

My poor father.

"Come, Papa," I say to him, "come to my wedding." He, like me, would rather have gone to bed.

Was it worth while to make friends with such high-class people?

I arrived very late at my fiancée's house to find a whole synhedrion already gathered there.

Too bad I'm not Veronese.

Around the long table, the great rabbi, a wise old man, a trifle crafty, a few big, imposing-looking bourgeois, a whole Pleiad of humble Jews, whose insides crisped as they waited for my arrival and . . . for the marriage feast. For without me there would have been no marriage feast. I knew it and I was amused at their agitation.

That this is the most important night in my life, that soon, without music, without stars and without sky, against the yellow background of the wall, under a red baldaquin, I shall be married—what do those gluttons care!

And I, as that solemn hour draws near, turn pale in the midst of the crowd.

Seated, standing, parents, friends, acquaintances, servants, came and went.

For them tears, smiles, confetti were already ripening. All that is proper to lavish on the fiancé.

They waited for me and, as they waited, they gossiped.

They were embarrassed to acknowledge that "he" was an artist.

Besides, it seems he's already famous . . . And he even gets money for his pictures. Did you know that?

"Nevertheless, that's no way to earn a living," sighs another.

"What are you saying? What about the fame and the honor?"

"But, after all, who is his father?" a third man wants to know.

"Ah! I know." They fall silent.

It seemed to me if they had put me in a coffin, my features would have been more supple, less rigid, than that mask that sat beside my future wife.

How I regretted that stupid timidity which prevented me from enjoying the mountain of grapes and fruits, the innumerable savory dishes that decorated the vast marriage table.

After half an hour (what am I saying? much before that) the synhedrion was in a hurry, blessings, wine, or perhaps curses rained down on our heads framed in the red baldaquin.

I thought I was going to faint. Everything whirled around me.

Deeply moved, I squeezed my wife's slender, bony hands. I wanted to run off with her to the country, to take her in my arms, to burst out laughing.

But after the nuptial benediction, my brothers-in-law led me to my house, while their sister, my wife, remained in her parents' home.

125   That was the height of ritual perfection.

At last, we are alone in the country.

Woods, pines, solitude. The moon behind the forest. The pig in the stable, the horse outside the window, in the fields. The sky lilac.

It was not only a honeymoon, but even more a milk-moon.

Not far from us a herd of cows belonging to the army was pastured. Every morning, soldiers sold pails-full of milk for a few kopeks. My wife, who had been brought up chiefly on cakes, gave me the milk to drink. With the result that, by autumn, I could scarcely button my coats.

As noon approached, our bedroom looked like one of those inspired panels in the great salons of Paris.

I was the winner. I chased a mouse that lept triumphantly up my easel. At that my wife thought: So he really is capable of killing something.

But the war rumbled over us. And Europe was closed to me.

I fumble in my pockets for my Paris certificate and I hurry to the governor of the town to ask his permission to leave.

Sadly, I come out with my papers stamped, sealed.

I felt as if I were covered with a long beard, or with fur, or as if I were quite naked.

My Paris!

What does the governor know about painting!

Trains filled to overflowing with soldiers. Broad faces with high cheekbones, gray and dusty.

They clung to the steps and climbed on the roofs of the cars.

They were off to Sebez, to Mohileff, they were moving closer to the front.

Why don't they call me?

I still have to wait my turn.

And what shall I do down there?

Look at the fields, the trees, the sky, the clouds, human blood and guts?

To all appearances they wanted nothing to do with me. I'm not reliable, I'm good for nothing, I don't even have any flesh on my bones. Colors, yes, a little pink on my cheeks, blue in my eyes, all that doesn't make a soldier.

Soldiers, moujiks in woolen caps, with *laptis* on their feet, pass in front of me. They eat, they stink. The smell of the front, the strong odor of herring, tobacco, lice.

I hear, I feel, the battles, the cannonading, the soldiers buried in the trenches.

The first prisoners arrive.

Here is a big German of athletic build, with a beard several months old; he is sullen and sleepy.

If it weren't wartime, I'd have stopped him and asked for news of Walden, of my pictures bottled up in Germany.

Another wounded man looks at me with an air of reproach. He is pale. He is old and thin, like my bearded grandfather.

13

What should I do? Meanwhile, I had to settle down somewhere.

In Petrograd, perhaps?

To tell the truth, I wasn't eager to go there. In the
country where we spent the summer, lived the great Rabbi
Schneersohn.

The inhabitants from all the region round about came
to consult him. Each one with his troubles.

Some wanted to get out of military service and came
to ask his advice. Others, disappointed at not having children, implored his blessing. Some people, bewildered by
a passage in the Talmud, asked for explanations. Or else
they simply came to see him, to be near him. How do I
know?

But certainly no artist had ever been registered on the
list of his visitors.

My God! Bewildered, but at a loss to choose a place to
live, I too ventured to ask advice of this scholarly rabbi
(I remember the rabbi's songs my mother used to sing on
Sabbath evenings).

Was he a real saint?

In summer, he lived in the country and his house
reminded one of an old synagogue, surrounded by mezza-
nines, by annexes for his followers and his personnel.

On reception days his antechamber was full of people.

They pushed and shoved each other amid a hubbub of
noise and gossiping.

However, for a good tip you got in more easily.

The porter gave me to understand that the rabbi did
not converse with ordinary mortals. I must put everything

in writing and hand him the note the moment I crossed the threshold.

No explanations.

At last, my turn having come, the door was opened before me and, shoved by that antheap of human beings, I find myself in a vast green drawing room.

Square, almost empty, silent.

At the far end, a long table littered with notes, sheets of paper, requests, prayers, money. The rabbi is the only one seated.

A candle flares. He skims through the note.

"So, you would like to go to Petrograd, my son? You think you will like it there. So be it, my son, I bless you. Go there."

"But, Rabbi," I say, "I'd rather stay in Vitebsk. You know, my parents and my wife's parents live there. . . ."

"Very well, my son, since you prefer Vitebsk, I bless you, go there."

I should like to have talked at greater length with him.

So many questions were burning my tongue.

I wanted to talk about art in general and mine in particular. Perhaps he would instill into me a little of the divine spirit. Who knows?

And to ask him if the Israelites are really the chosen people of God, as it says in the Bible. And to know, moreover, what he thought about Christ, whose pale face had been troubling me for a long time.

Without a backward glance I reached the door and went out.

I ran to my wife. It was moonlight. The dogs barked. And there was nothing half so good as. . . .

My God! What sort of a rabbi are you, Rabbi Schneer-sohn!

Since that time, whatever advice I am given, I do exactly the opposite. I could simply have stayed in that village where I would have blindly followed that same rabbi, who was returning to his headquarters in the little suburb of Lubawitchy.

But the war intervened and my class was called up. . . .

What should I do? My wife preferred big cities. She loves culture. She is right.

Doesn't she have enough trouble with me? I shall never understand why men crowd together in the same places when, outside of cities, tens of thousands of empty miles stretch right and left.

I'd be satisfied with some sort of a hole, a secluded nook. I'd be happy there.

I would sit down in a synagogue and I would look. Just that. Or on a bench beside a river or else I would pay visits. And I'd paint, I'd paint pictures which, perhaps, would surprise the whole world.

No.

One fine evening (it's always a fine evening), a rainy evening, I climb, in my turn, into a train crawling with soldiers, all cursing and fighting for a seat.

With difficulty I manage to cling to the steps. The train starts off. I press against a back, hanging on to the shoulders of another soldier. The train pulls out.

The jokers, at the back, swell out their bodies and hand out advice.

"Give him (they're talking about me) a punch and that'll be enough."

One shove from their backs laden with packs and I would shoot like an arrow into the dark and snowy fields.

I grip the ramps harder, my hands are freezing. I fly, and the train flies with me.

My coat billows out in the wind like a parachute and flaps in the cold.

In this way I arrive in Petrograd. What's the use?

There I found the haven the war had reserved for me —a military office. That's where I scribbled on paper.

My chief made war on me. As he was my brother-in-law, he was always afraid of being called down for my inefficiency so he kept a particularly close watch on me.

He would come up to me and ask for certain information. Alas! As I was almost never able to give it to him, he would sweep all the papers off my desk and shout, furiously:

"Well, then, what kind of method do you have? What have you done? Is it possible, Marc Zacharovitch, you didn't know even that? And yet it's a mere trifle! . . ."

When I saw him in such a rage, eyes and cheeks aflame, I felt sorry for him.

To myself, I smiled.

However, in the end he managed to inculcate in me a new talent; from that time I knew, after a fashion, how to handle records, both incoming and outgoing. I even cooked up some reports.

Compared to my military bureau, the front seemed to me like a promenade, like exercises in the open air.

Towards evening I returned to my home, sad.

I could almost have cried.

I poured out my sufferings to my wife. She suffered in silence.

I was glad when, on certain evenings, I could do at least a little painting and talk about it with my friend, the doctor-author, Baal-Machschowess-Eljacheff.

His friendship was a joy to me, especially at that time.

We had met at the house of the collector Kagan Schabschay, where art was passionately discussed.

That collector was one of the first to buy several of my pictures for the purpose of founding a national museum.

Every evening we went out with Eljacheff; as we wandered through the narrow side-streets of Moscow, he talked brilliantly, eloquently.

When he turned towards me abruptly in the dark his glasses shone.

His little black mustache, his sharp, penetrating glance, held my eyes.

At once skeptical and kindly, he listened, talked, argued, waving his arms and limping slightly.

We became great friends.

And if, occasionally, I chanced to spend the night at his house, he talked till morning, by the faint light of the night-lamp beside my bed. He talked to me of writers, war, life in general, of art, revolution, his nephew, of the People's Commissar and, especially, of his wife who had left him.

He had met her when she was very young. She was an extremely beautiful girl: black eyes, a *mat* complexion, tall and slender, and as silent as if she were a statue.

Neither my friend's writing, nor his love touched her.

Indifferent, she accepted his favors coldly. And one fine day she left him to go off with another man.

"You understand," my friend said to me, "she needed a man who could satisfy her completely. Just look at me: one side paralyzed and when I talk, I slobber."

In the forenoons he waited for patients—in vain.

Then he began to write.

More than once, in those years of cold and hunger, he shared with us his ration of horse meat. We feasted on it in his kitchen, with his little son playing nearby. He was bringing up the boy as best he could.

Holding a glass of tea between his trembling hands, he talks, talks, talks. His tea spills; it is cold by this time. I drink mine and he, still talking, adjusts his glasses that have nearly fallen into the tea, chilled between his frozen hands.

I showed my pictures to another friend too, to the venerable Syrkine.

He was so nearsighted he had to use a pair of binoculars to see anything and when he met you, he bumped into you.

He stood up for me with real devotion.

Where are you today?

14

The Germans carried off their first victories. Poison gases choked me even at Liteiny Prospect 46, headquarters of my military bureau.

My painting grew dull.

One very dark evening, I went out alone. The street was deserted. The cobblestones in the road stood out distinctly.

It seems there's a pogrom in the center of town.

A gang of hoodlums have gone into action.

Wearing military coats, with epaulettes and buttons ripped off, that suspect gang roamed the streets amusing themselves by throwing passers-by into the water from the top of the bridge. You could hear shooting.

I was curious to see that pogrom close at hand.

I move forward quietly. The street lights are out. I feel panicky, especially in front of butchers' windows. There, you can see calves still alive, lying beside the butcher's hatchets and knives. Locked up for their last night, they bleat piteously.

Suddenly, around the corner, comes a gang of four or five looters, armed to the teeth. The moment they catch sight of me they ask:

"Jew or not?"

For a second, I hesitate. It is dark.

My pockets are empty, my fingers sensitive, my legs weak and they are thirsty for blood. My death will be of no use. I wanted so much to live.

"All right! Get along!" they shout.

Without a moment's hesitation I run towards the center of town where the pogrom started.

Gunshots. Bodies falling into the water.
I run home.

I prayed that Wilhelm might be satisfied with Warsaw, with Kowno! Don't come to Dvinsk! And above all,
don't touch Vitebsk! That's where I am and I'm painting
my pictures.

But Wilhelm was lucky, the Russians fought badly.
Though they fought furiously, they couldn't drive out their
enemy. Our people are excellent only in attack.

Each setback to the Army was an excuse for its chief,
the Grand Duke Nicholas Nicolaevitch, to blame the Jews.

"Get them all out in twenty-four hours. Or have them
shot. Or both at once."

The army was advancing, and as they advanced, the
Jewish population retreated *en masse,* abandoning cities
and villages.

I longed to put them down on my canvases, to get them
out of harm's way.

Clenched hands were raised threateningly to the skies.

Soldiers fled from the front. War, ammunitions, lice,
everything is left behind in the trenches.

Seized with panic, soldiers break car windows, take
the demolished trains by assault and, piling in like her-
rings, rush towards the cities, towards the capital.

Freedom roared in their mouths. Oaths hissed.

I don't stay, either. I desert my office, inkwell, and all
the records. Good-bye!

I, too, along with the others, quit the front.

Freedom and the end of the war.

Freedom. Freedom for all.

135   The February revolution breaks out.

My first feeling is one of relief that I'll never have to bother with the passport man again. The Volunsky regiment was the first to revolt.

I ran to Znamensky Square, from there to Liteiny, to Nevsky and back again.

On all sides rifle fire. Guns were made ready. Arms put in order.

"Hurrah for the Duma! Hurrah for the Provisional Government!"

The artillerymen voted for the people. With horses and cannon they started off. The other corps, one after the other, swear allegiance. After them, officers, sailors.

In front of the Duma, President Rodzianko thunders:

"Don't forget, my brothers, the enemy is still at your gates! Swear! Swear allegiance!"

"We swear! Hurrah!"

They were hoarse from shouting.

Something was about to be born.

I was living in an almost semi-conscious state.

I had never even heard of Kerensky. He was at the peak of his glory. Hand on chest, like Napoleon, the same piercing glance too. He sleeps in the Imperial bed.

The Constitutional Democratic ministry is followed by the ministry of semi-Democrats. After them, the Democrats. They joined forces. Checkmate.

After that, General Korniloff tried to save Russia. Deserters attacked the entire railway system.

"Let's go home!"

It was June. The Revolutionary Socialist Party was in

favor at the moment. Tchernoff made speeches at the amphitheatre of the circus.

"Constituent Assembly, Constituent Assembly!"

On Znamensky Square in front of the great monument of Alexander III, people began to whisper:

"Lenin has arrived."

"Who's he?"

"Lenin from Geneva?"

"The very same."

"He's here."

"Is it possible?"

"Down with him! Drive him out! Hurrah for the Provisional Government! All power to the Constituent Assembly!"

"Is it true he came from Germany in a sealed train?"

At the Michailovsky Theatre, actors and painters have gathered together. They intend to found a Ministry of Arts.

I am present as a spectator.

Suddenly, among the names suggested by the younger group for minister, I hear my name.

I leave Petrograd and return to my Vitebsk. I still prefer my home town to being a minister.

When she saw me neglect my painting, my wife wept. She warned me it would all end badly.

That was what happened.

Unfortunately she is always right.

When will I learn to take her advice?

15

Russia was almost covered with ice.

Lenin turned it upside down the way I turn my pictures.

Madame Kchessinsky has left. Lenin is making a speech from his balcony.

Everyone is there. The letters R.S.F.S.R. are already turning red. The factories are shut down.

Horizons opened up.

Space and emptiness.

No more bread. The black headlines on the morning posters made me sick at heart.

Coup d'état. Lenin, president of the Sovnarkom. Lunacharsky, president of the Narkompross.

Trotsky is there too. Also Zinovieff. Uritzky guards the entrances of the Constituent Assembly.

They're all there and I . . . I'm at Vitebsk.

I can go without food for several days, sit beside a mill and look at the bridge, the beggars, the unfortunates, laden with bundles.

I can linger in front of the bathhouses and see soldiers and their women come out carrying birch switches in their hands.

I can wander along the river bank, near the cemetery . . .

I can forget you, Vladimir Ilyitch, you, Lenin, as well as Trotsky . . .

And in place of all that, instead of peacefully painting my pictures, I have founded a School of Fine Arts and have become its director, its president and everything else.

"What luck!"

"What madness!" thought my wife.

The Narkom, Lunacharsky, receives me with a smile in his private office in the Kremlin.

I met him once in Paris, shortly before the war. He was a journalist. He came to my studio, in "La Ruche."

Glasses, a little goatee, the mask of a faun.

He came to look at my pictures and write an article about them in a newspaper.

I've heard he's a Marxist. But my knowledge of Marxism is confined to knowing that Marx was a Jew and that he had a long white beard. Now, I realized that, without a doubt, my art would not find favor with him.

I said to Lunacharsky:

"Above all, don't ask me why I painted blue or green and why a calf is visible in the cow's belly, etc. Anyway, let Marx, if he's so wise, come to life and explain it to you."

I showed him my canvases, rushing through them at top speed.

He smiled and silently took notes.

I have the feeling he has kept a bad memory of that visit, and will always have it.

And now he is solemnly confirming me in my new functions.

I return to Vitebsk on the eve of the first anniversary of the October revolution.

My town, like all the others, is getting ready to celebrate by decorating its streets with huge posters.

In our town there are quite a few house-painters.

I gathered them all together, young and old, and I told them:

"Listen: you and your children will all be pupils in my school.

"Shut up your workshops for signs and daubs. All orders will be transmitted to our school and you will divide them among yourselves.

"Here are a dozen sketches. Copy them on large canvases and the day the workers' parade comes through town, with its flags and torches, you are to cover the walls of the town and the suburbs with these canvases."

All the house-painters, the old bearded fellows as well as their apprentices, began to copy my cows and my horses. And on October 25, throughout the town, my multicolored animals swung back and forth, swollen with revolution.

The workers marched forward singing the International.

When I saw their smiles I was sure they understood me.

Their Communist leaders appeared to be less satisfied.

Why is the cow green and why is the horse flying in the sky? Why?

What has that to do with Marx and Lenin?

There was a rush to place orders with the young sculptors for busts of Lenin and Marx, in cement.

I'm afraid they melted under the rains of Vitebsk.

Poor city!

When they set up, in the public park, that timid cast done by a pupil of my school, I hid behind the bushes and grinned.

Wherever is Marx? Where is he?

Where is the bench on which I kissed you once upon a time?

Where can I sit to hide my shame?

One Marx was not enough.

On another street they had set up still another one.

It was not any more fortunate than the first.

Big and heavy, it was even less benevolent and frightened the coachmen whose cab-stands were just across the way.

I was ashamed. Was it my fault?

Dressed in a Russian blouse, with a leather case under my arm, I certainly looked like a Soviet official.

Only my long hair and, on my cheeks, a few pink spots that had rubbed off from my pictures, betrayed the painter.

My eyes glowed with administrative fire. I was surrounded by young boys—pupils I'm preparing to turn into geniuses in twenty-four hours.

I wear myself out struggling to obtain the subsidies the school needs, to procure money, paints, material. I make the most strenuous efforts to get them out of their military service.

I was constantly on the go, running here and there. In my absence, my wife replaced me.

I attended the Goubispolkom meetings to solicit money from the town.

While I was explaining my project, the president of the soviet purposely fell asleep.

He didn't wake up till the end of my speech and then he asked:

"Which do you think the more important, Comrade Chagall, to have an emergency repair done to the bridge or to allocate money to your Academy of Fine Arts?"

Each time that, thanks to Lunacharsky's backing, I received grants, he demanded that I should at least submit to his authority. If not, he threatened me with prison.

But I never consented to that.

From time to time other commissars came to see me. To remind myself that they were only boys putting on airs and trying to make themselves important by pounding the table during conferences, I used to amuse myself by giving the military commissar, an adolescent of nineteen, or the commissar of public works, a few whacks on the back or on the behind. Though they were husky lads, especially the former, they quickly admitted defeat and I sat down triumphantly on the military commissar's back.

All that emphasized the respect the city authorities had for the arts. Which did not, however, prevent them from arresting my mother-in-law, along with all the other bourgeois, simply because they were wealthy.

Among the various calls I was obliged to make, I had occasion to go to Maxim Gorky's house.

I don't know what he thought of me.

As I entered his house, I noticed on the walls, pictures so lacking in taste that I thought I had got into the wrong place.

He was lying in bed and spitting, now into his handkerchief, now into a spittoon.

He accepted all my plans with a look of surprise, but

offered no objections; as he looked at me I knew he was trying to guess where I came from and who I was.

And I had forgotten what I had come to ask of him.

To me it was enough for a man to express a desire, and taking pity on him, I would promptly invite him to become a professor in my school. For I was eager to have all tendencies in art represented there.

One man, whom I had even appointed director, spent his time sending food packages to his family. At the post office, and even in the Communist Committee, they began to talk about those professors invited by Comrade Chagall.

One of the women I had appointed amused herself by flirting with the two commissars, willingly accepting their favors. When this was reported to me, I was furious.

"How is that possible?" I demanded feverishly. But she answered slyly:

"Why, Comrade Chagall, I do it for your sake! . . . to help you."

A third professor, who lived in the academy proper, surrounded himself with women in the throes of "suprematique" mysticism.

What means he used to attract them, I do not know.

Another, my most zealous disciple, swore friendship and devotion to me. To hear him, I was his Messiah. But the moment he was appointed professor, he went over to my opponents' camp and heaped insults and ridicule on me.

He had already begun to worship a new god whom, in turn, he hastened to betray.

Then there was an old friend, a schoolmate.

I had called him to my side as my assistant. He was working in some sort of office.

What's the point of it, I thought; he's wasting his time there.

I took him with me.

He was very glad and, to show his gratitude he, too, lost no time in going over to my enemies.

As president I was obliged to hold meetings late into the night. Passionately I urged the professors to live up to their duties; but little by little they nodded and fell asleep.

They made all manner of fun of those meetings, of the school itself, of myself and my convictions.

It is true, I didn't have much patience. I would let them have the floor, but as I knew in advance what they were going to say, I would never let them finish. I wanted to bring academy, museum and communal ateliers into being all at once.

I was impatient to see everything working. And I neither rested, nor let the others rest.

As all the professors "doted on" one another, they began to "dote on" me too.

I became a celebrity in the town and I turned out dozens of painters.

16

One day when I was away, trying as usual to get bread, paints and money for them, all those professors rebelled and drew my pupils into their rebellion.

May God forgive them!

Backed by all those whom I had procured for them, and now assured of bread and employment, they posted a notice, expelling me from the school within twenty-four hours.

As soon as I had left, they immediately calmed down.

There was no one left to fight with. After taking over all the school property, even to pictures I had bought from them on behalf of the State with the intention of founding a museum in Vitebsk, they scattered, abandoning school and pupils to the hazards of fate.

That makes me laugh. What's the use of digging up all that old stuff?

I shan't say any more about friends and enemies.

Their features are sunk into my heart like logs of wood.

Make me leave within twenty-four hours, with all my family!

Make me take down my signs, my notices—stutter as much as you please!

Don't worry, I shan't remember you.

Nor do I want you to remember me either.

When, neglecting my own work for several years, I devoted myself entirely to the needs of my native land, it was not for love of you, but for my town, for my father, for my mother, who lie buried there.

As for the rest of you, let me alone.

145   I shan't be surprised if, after I have been absent a long time, my town obliterates all traces of me and forgets the man who, laying aside his own paint brushes, worried, suffered and took the trouble to implant Art there, who dreamed of making ordinary houses into museums and the average citizen into a creator.

And I understood then that no man is a prophet in his own country.

I went to Moscow.

I think of friends. Were they really friends?

My first childhood friend, whom I loved dearly, left me, dropping me as effortlessly as a piece of gauze comes away from a wound.

And why?

While still a pupil in the School of Fine Arts, he helped himself to my class drawings, rubbed out my signature and passed them off as his own. I didn't reproach him. But the management nevertheless fired him.

Later, when I was living in Paris, he vowed he would take my fiancée away from me and he tried to win her by pretending a devotion he did not feel.

And finally, when he saw the canvases of my adult years, and no longer understood me, he became jealous like all the others.

In this way our childhood friendship died out on the threshold of ugly, adult life.

It wasn't even a friendship; he wasn't a friend.

With whom then shall I make friends? Whom shall I love?

So now my doors are open.

My soul too, even my smile, sometimes.

I'm no longer surprised when people drop me, when I'm betrayed, and I no longer enjoy newcomers. I'm on my guard.

No friends. Another one has also left me. He is not poor now, he is even famous.

But the world is filled with friends.

When it snows I open my mouth to swallow it.

Is that it?

That's what friends are.

May God help me to shed real tears only before my canvases!

There my wrinkles, my pale face will remain fixed; there my fluid soul will be imprinted forever.

My town is dead. The Vitebsk course is run!

All my relatives are dead.

I shall write a few words for myself alone.

You may leave them unread. Turn away.

My sisters! It is dreadful not to have put up a monument yet for papa, nor for Rosine, nor for David. Write to me at once, we'll come to an agreement. If not, we shall end by forgetting where each one lies.

My memory is on fire.

I made a sketch of you, David, with your mandolin in your hand. You were laughing. Your rosy mouth, showing all your teeth. You are blue in my picture.

You lie in the Crimea, in foreign soil, in that place you drew so painstakingly from your hospital window. My heart lies there with you.

My dear father . . .

The longing of our last years tears me apart and my

canvases quiver under those blasts. My father loaded trucks: he scarcely earned his living. An auto knocked him down, crushed him and killed him outright.

They hid the letter anouncing his death from me. Why?

And yet I almost never cry. I did not go back to Vitebsk.

And therefore I witnessed neither Mama's death, nor Papa's.

I couldn't have endured it.

As it is, I feel life too keenly. To see, in addition, that "truth" with my own eyes . . . to lose the last illusion . . . I can't.

But perhaps that would help me.

I would have seen the features of my parents in death, my mother's face, her dead face, all white.

She loved me so dearly. Where was I? Why didn't I go? It isn't right.

And my father's face, crushed by destiny and by the wheels of an automobile. It's wicked that I wasn't there. He would have been so pleased if I had appeared. But he will not come to life again.

I shall see your grave later. It is two feet from Mama's grave. I shall lie down full length on your grave. You will not come to life even then. And when I am old (or perhaps before) I shall lie near you.

Enough of Vitebsk. It is finished.

A period to its art.

Only you—you are with me. The only one, of whom my soul will not speak in vain.

148　　When I gaze earnestly at you, it seems to me that you are my work.

More than once you saved my canvases from a melancholy fate.

I do not understand men, any more than my pictures. Everything you say is right. Then guide my hand. Take the paintbrush and, like the leader of an orchestra, carry me off to far and unknown regions.

May our late parents bless the conception of our painting. Let black be black and white even whiter.

And our little girl is with us. Forgive me, darling, for not remembering you sooner, for not coming to see you until four days after you were born.

It is shameful. I had dreamed of a boy. . . .

17

Idotchka is born. Almost immediately after her birth, we took her to the country.

A newborn babe is not a fragile vase. My wife wrapped her from head to foot so that she would not take cold.

I said to her: "I think you should at least leave her mouth free; a human being needs air."

At last, we arrived. And as soon as we unwrapped that infant bundle, we cried out at the same time as the babe, who, furious with rage, was puffing like a volcano.

"You see?"

My sister and her husband were our neighbors. At every step their baby left a trail behind him. So, all day long, the floor was stained. And the chamber pots, to be sure!

In the bedroom, a single window.

You could see the end of the road and a pine in the middle. But my brother-in-law sat down in front of it and hid the view from me.

Idotchka refused to take sugared water.

The drops of milk had become rare. Certainly they were very tasty, for, though we did not sweeten her water, she wasn't fooled a bit.

She yelled so loud I couldn't keep from dumping her furiously on her bed.

"Shut up!"

I can't stand children's piercing cries. It's frightful!

In short, I'm not paternal.

People will say I'm a monster.

I'm losing their respect.

What's the use of writing all that?

And later! Do you remember, my darling, what happened, a few years afterwards in Malachowka?

I had a dream: a little bitch bit our Idotchka. It was night. Through my bedroom window I saw the vault of the sky crossed by gigantic, multicolored squares, by rounds, meridians, streaked with written signs.

Moscow, stop: Berlin, stop: New York, stop. Rembrandt, Vitebsk. Millions of agonies.

All the colors, except ultramarine, smoulder and burn.

I turn around and I see my picture in which men are beside themselves, frantic.

It was hot. Everything looked green.

I lie between those two worlds, looking out of the window. The sky is not blue now and at night it sings like a seashell and shines more brilliantly than the sun.

Could that dream have been a portent of my dash across fields the next day when my little girl fell and was hurt?

Crying, bleeding from the wound where a little stick had pierced her cheek, she ran towards me with all her might.

And again I feel that everything twists and turns inside me, that I'm even walking strangely over the ground.

If I could write, the pellets of my words would be flatter than the earth of that field where you fell, my darling little one.

It seems to me that after me everything will be different.

And this world of ours, will it be alive?

18

However, my pupils have repented. They are urging me to come back to my school. They have drawn up a petition, assuring me that they need me.

They swear to obey me, etc.

Here I am again with my family, in a freight train, along with the pram, the samovar, and other household objects.

My soul, like a damp room, sweats slowly.

Hope hides in my leather portfolio.

There, too, is my judgment and the solid basis of all my illusions.

It's snowing. It's cold. No wood.

They have installed me in two rooms that are part of an apartment occupied by a large Polish family. Their looks pierce you, like swords.

"Just you wait. The Poles will come to Vitebsk soon and they'll kill your father," the children say to my little girl.

Meanwhile we are being furiously attacked by flies.

We live very near the barracks. From there, thousands of flies swarm up joyously, fly gaily down the street and force their way into our apartment through every crack and cranny. They sting pictures, faces, arms, furniture, my wife and my child, so thoroughly that she falls ill.

Soldiers walk past our windows. Dirty boys in rags play in front of our door, and my daughter, filled with pity, presents them with our silver spoons and forks.

I change lodgings again. A rich old man ventures to give us asylum in the hope that, as director of the Academy, I shall be in a position to protect him. From what?

As a matter of fact, they leave him alone.

That lonely, miserly old man feeds himself like a sick dog. His cook blows into the empty casseroles and smiles, waiting for him to die.

No one goes to see him. Outside, the revolution is going on. He has no idea of it. His sole concern is to look out for his property.

He sits alone at his large table.

The hanging lamp, brightly lighted during his wife's lifetime, gives scarcely any light now and its dim shadow outlines his bent shoulders and twisted arms, his beard and his yellow, wrinkled face.

He has nothing to do.

At night when the soldiers of the Cheka come to search his house, they have to pass through our bedroom.

They stop first to question me.

I show my papers. They read them and smile.

"And in there?"

"In there lives an old man so ancient that the moment you go up to him he'll fall dead. Will you risk that?"

And they go away.

In that way I saved him more than once, until at last he died a natural death.

That was the end of my apartment. Where was I to find lodgings?

Long before this time, the house of my parents-in-law had been destroyed.

One afternoon, seven cars belonging to the Cheka drew up in front of the dazzling show-windows and soldiers began to gather up precious stones, gold, silver, watches, everything in the three shops. They even entered the apartment to see if there was anything of value there.

They even carried off, from the kitchen, the silver service that had just been cleared from the table.

Afterwards, they went up to my mother-in-law and, thrusting a revolver under her nose:

"The keys of the strongbox, or else . . ."

As they either did not know how to open the strong-boxes, or else respected their value, they loaded them, too, with much effort into their cars.

At last, satisfied, they left.

My wife's parents, who seemed suddenly to have aged, sat mute, arms hanging at their sides, eyes staring towards that distance into which the seven cars were disappearing.

The crowd that had gathered wept silently.

They had carried off everything. Not even one spoon was left.

That evening, the family sent the maid out to look for some ordinary spoons.

The father takes his, lifts it to his mouth, puts it down. Tears stream down on the pewter spoon and mingle with his tea.

At night the Chekists came back, armed with guns and shovels.

"House search!"

With the aid of an "expert," an envious enemy, they broke through walls and ripped up floors. They were searching for hidden treasures.

That was enough to break down the courage of my wife's parents, though they were accustomed to frequent aggressions and outrages from ordinary thieves, tempted by their conspicuous fortune.

Moscow, surrounded by the Kremlin, or the Kremlin surrounded by Moscow, by the Soviets.

Hungry mouths and the howling of October.

Who am I? A writer, eh? Is it for me to describe how in these years our muscles stiffen?

The flesh turned into colors; the body to a paintbrush and the head to a tower.

I put on my wide trousers, my yellow smock (presents from Americans who, out of pity for us, sent us their old clothes), and like everyone else, I went to the meetings.

There were a great many.

Foreign policy meetings presided over by Lunacharsky; theatrical meetings; meetings of poets, of artists.

Which should one choose?

Meyerhold, with a red scarf around his neck and the profile of an exiled emperor, is the mainstay of the theatrical revolution.

Not so long ago he worked at the Imperial Theatre, and wore the uniform ostentatiously.

I like him alone among them all. I'm even sorry I've never worked with him.

Poor Tairoff, so eager for novelties that come to him third hand. Meyerhold gave him no peace.

And there was no better show than their frequent squabbles.

At the poets' meeting, Mayakowsky shouts the loudest.

Though he had written a dedication to me in one of his books: "God grant that everyone may *chagalle** like Chagall!," we were not friends.

---

* *Chagalle:* the Russian word for "march forward."

He realized that his shouting and his spitting in public disgusted me.

Does poetry need such fuss and noise?

I preferred Essenine, whose broad smile touched me.

He shouted too, drunk with God, not with wine. With tears in his eyes, he pounded, not on the table but on his breast, and spat, not on others, but on himself.

From the speaker's platform, he waved to me.

His poetry may not be perfect, but is it not, after Block's, the only cry of the soul in Russia?

And what could I do at the painter's meeting?

There, pupils of yesterday, friends of other days, neighbors, control the art of all Russia.

They look at me distrustfully and pityingly.

But I have no pretensions now and besides, I am not invited now as professor.

Who, except me, is not a professor nowadays?

Here is one of the leaders of the "Bubnovy Valet" group.

Pointing to a lamppost in the center of the Kremlin Square, he adds maliciously:

"That's where they'll hang the lot of you."

It seems that meanwhile he is an extremely zealous revolutionary.

Another man, whom God deprived of talent, raises this cry: "Down with painting!"

The "successful" artists of Czarist days glare at him resentfully.

In the distance I see my old friend, Tugendhold, who was one of the first to speak of me.

Now he is as fascinated by proletarian art, and just as obstinately as he was formerly by Western art.

156   A would-be artist speaks disdainfully of painting, about which he knows nothing. Finally, gazing lovingly at a chair before him, he exclaims:

"Now, my wife and I shall do nothing but paint chairs."

A new revelation, like the "discoveries" of Cubism, Simultaneism, Constructivism, *contre-relief,* brought back from Europe ten years after!

And they end by "revealing themselves" again in academism.

But, when I heard someone shout: "I don't give a damn about your soul. I need your legs, not your head," I hesitated no longer.

Enough! I want to keep my soul.

And I think that the revolution can be great while at the same time retaining respect for others.

Had I only been a little bolder, I, like so many others, could have obtained a number of privileges. But no.

I stammer and stutter, I'm always diffident.

I am looking for lodgings in Moscow. I've had enough of Vitebsk.

At last I found a little room, overlooking the courtyard. Damp. In the bed even the blankets are damp. The baby lies in dampness. Pictures turn yellow. The walls seem to run.

What's this! Am I in prison?

A bundle of wood is spread out at the foot of the bed.

I had a hard time getting it.

"The wood is dry," the sly peasant assured me. But where to find someone to saw it?

Impossible to carry those huge logs up to the fifth floor and I wouldn't risk leaving them outside—they would all be stolen.

Four soldiers whom I met by chance, helped me drag armloads of wood upstairs to our bedroom and stow them crosswise as if the room were a hangar.

At night, you would have said a whole forest had begun to thaw. The pines run and drip, drip, drip.

Are there wolves between those logs, foxes with long tails?

It was as though we were sleeping out of doors, as though we were hearing the sound of water dripping, of snow melting.

All that was lacking were the clouds of Moscow, and the moon.

Nevertheless we slept and dreamed.

On awakening my wife urged me:

"Go and look at the baby. Is there much snow in her bed? Cover her mouth!"

No money. We didn't need any—there was nothing to buy.

I am given rations and I drag them over the icy road, like a mass of white wings mixed with raw meat, red, bony.

What can we do with it? A whole half of a cow. A whole bag of flour. Hurrah for the mice!

I like herring, but herring every day! I like kasha made from millet. But every day!

Then too, we had to have a little butter and milk for the baby.

My wife takes her jewels to the Soucharewska market,

but the market is blocked off and the militia arrest her.

"In the name of God," she begs, "let me go. My baby is home, alone. I am only trying to exchange my rings for a little butter."

I am not complaining. I was all right. What did it matter?

A kind man took us into his apartment. We all slept in the same room, my wife, the child, the nurse and I.

The stove smokes. The pipes drip dampness on the beds. Tears of joy harden in eyes filled with smoke. In one corner of the room the snow glints like an innocent roll of cotton.

The wind is gentle and the crackling of the fire sounds, at a distance, like loud kisses.

We are happy and empty.

Smiles crease my face and the black Soviet bread I put in my mouth, seems to burden my heart.

At night our host shared his flat with two girls. Thus he consoled himself.

In times of famine, in the days of the Soviets! You bourgeois!

In exasperation, I flung myself eagerly into my work on the ceiling and walls of the Moscow theatre.

There, in obscurity, my mural paintings sigh. Have you seen them?

Rant and rave, my contemporaries!

No matter how, my first theatrical ABC's gave you a bellyful.

Not modest, eh? Tell that to my grandmother; modesty bores me.

Despise me, if you wish.

19

"There you are," said Efross as he led me into a dark room, "these walls are at your disposal. Do with them what you please."

It was a completely demolished apartment that had once belonged to bourgeois refugees.

"You see," he continued, "here are benches for the audience; there, the stage."

To tell the truth, I saw nothing but the remains of a kitchen over there, and here . . .

"Down with the old theatre that stinks of garlic and sweat. Hurrah . . ."

And I flung myself at the walls.

The canvases were stretched out on the floor. Workmen, actors walked over them.

Rooms and corridors were in the process of being repaired; piles of shavings mingled with my tubes of paint, with my sketches. At every step one dislodged cigarette butts, crusts of bread.

I, too, was stretched out on the floor.

There are times when I enjoy lying down in that position. At home we lay the dead man on the floor. His relatives, also on the floor, came and wept beside his bed.

I like to lie against the earth and whisper to it my sorrows, my prayers.

I remember a distant ancestor of mine who did the paintings in the Mohileff synagogue.

And I wept.

Why did he not call me, a hundred years ago, to help him? At least now, may he pray before the High Altar, may he protect me.

Distill in me, my bearded grandfather, one or two drops of eternal truth.

To console myself, I sent Effroim, the janitor of the theatre, to get me some bread and milk.

The milk wasn't real milk; the bread wasn't bread. Watery milk, with starch in it. Bread made of oats, of straw, the color of tobacco.

Perhaps it was real milk milked from a revolutionary cow. Or else the janitor had simply filled the pitcher with water, mixed heaven knows what with it, and served it to me like that, the wretch!

It was like white blood or even worse.

I ate, I drank, I was filled with enthusiasm.

That janitor, sole representative of the working class in our theatre, I can see him still.

His nose, his poverty, his weakness, his stupidity, his lice that hopped from him to me and back again. Often he just stood there, doing nothing and smiling nervously.

"What are you laughing at, idiot?"

"I don't know which to look at: your painting or you. One's as funny as the other!"

Effroim, where are you? Granted you were only a janitor, though sometimes by chance you did stand behind the ticket window and even checked tickets.

I often thought: we ought to put him on the stage. Why not? They hired the wife of the other janitor.

That woman's figure was like a cord of damp wood, covered with snow.

At rehearsals she shouted and ranted like a pregnant mare.

I wouldn't have wished her on my worst enemy.

Horrors!

Next door was the office of Director Granovsky. While the theatre was being repaired, little work went on there.

The room is narrow. He is in bed. On the floor, shavings. He pampers his body.

"How are you, Alexi Michailovitch?"

He lies there and smiles or else he sulks and grumbles. More than once, his cutting remarks were aimed at me or at other visitors.

I do not know whether Granovsky is still smiling now.

But like the milk the janitor brought me, his smile comforted me a little.

I never dared to ask him if he liked me.

And so I left without ever knowing.

To work for the theatre had long been my dream.

Even in 1911, Tugenhold had written somewhere that the objects on my canvases lived.

I could have painted psychological scenes, he said.

I have given some thought to that.

Indeed, a little later he advised the stage manager, Tairoff, to think of me for "The Merry Wives of Windsor."

We had a meeting with him and we separated—that was all.

My stay in Vitebsk coming to an end in 1919, after I had introduced arts and artists, friends and enemies there, I was delighted to receive an invitation from Granovsky and Efross. They asked me to come and work for the opening of the new Jewish theatre.

It is Efross who insisted upon inviting me.

Efross? Tremendously long legs. Neither noisy, nor

162 silent. Restless, constantly in motion. Everything shines: his glasses, his beard.

He is here, there, everywhere.

He is one of the friends I love and he deserves it.

Granovsky I heard of for the first time in Petersburg during the war.

A pupil of Reinhardt's, from time to time he put on huge productions which, after Reinhardt's "Oedipus" had visited Russia, enjoyed a certain vogue.

At the same time, he organized Jewish productions. His company was made up of men from all professions, with whom he founded his theatrical school.

I saw his productions, in the realistic style of Stanislavsky.

I did not conceal my dislike.

That is why, when I went to Moscow, I was worried.

I felt that, at least in the beginning, there would be no accord between us.

I, always anxious and worried about the least thing; he, confident, assured, given to mockery.

And—this is the essential point—not at all Chagall.

I had been asked to paint murals for the auditorium and scenery for the first production.

Ah! I thought, here is an opportunity to do away with the old Jewish theatre, its psychological naturalism, its false beards. There on these walls I shall at least be able to do as I please and be free to show everything I consider indispensable to the rebirth of the national theatre.

Had I not proposed taking out one of the actor Michoels' eyes to perfect his make-up?

I set to work.

I painted a mural for the main wall: Introduction to the New National Theatre.

The other interior walls, the ceiling and the friezes displayed the forerunners of the contemporary actor—a popular musician, a wedding jester, a woman dancing, a copyist of the Torah, the first poet dreamer, and finally a modern couple twirling over the stage. Dishes and food, beigels and fruit scattered on tables set for a feast, decorated the friezes.

I looked forward to meeting the actors.

To myself I silently implored the stage manager, the actors, who passed me:

"Let us agree. Let's join forces and get rid of all this old rubbish. Let's perform a miracle!"

The actors liked me. Often they would send me either a piece of bread or a little soup, or a smile, or hope.

At that moment Granovsky was going slowly through the renaissance of Reinhardt and Stanislavsky towards other horizons.

But when I was there, he was still living in other worlds.

I don't know why he never took me into his confidence. I dared not confide in him either.

It was the actor Michoels, famished like everyone else, who broke the ice.

More than once, he came up to me, eyes and forehead bulging, hair disheveled. A short nose, thick lips. He follows your thought attentively, anticipates it and, by the acute angle of his arms and his body, rushes towards the essential point. Unforgettable!

He looked at my painting, begged me to lend him my sketches. He wanted to get to know them, grow accustomed to them, and understand them.

One or two months later, he told me happily:

"You know, I've studied your sketches. I understand them. As a result I've changed my personality completely. From now on I know how to use my body in a different way, how to move, to speak."

"Everyone looks at me," he said, "and they can't understand what has happened."

In reply, I smiled. He smiled.

Other actors move forward cautiously towards my canvases, towards me, seated on top of the tall ladder; they try to see something, to understand.

Couldn't they, too, transform their ideas.

We lacked everything. No material for costumes and settings.

On the eve of the opening, they brought me old worn suits. I painted them hastily.

In the pockets I discovered cigarette butts, crusts of bread.

On the opening night I could not even appear in the auditorium, I was so splattered with colors. And only a few seconds before the curtain went up I ran across the floor of the stage to hastily paint in the properties. I could not stand "naturalism."

All of a sudden, opposition.

Granovsky had hung up a real dustcloth.

I sigh and shout:

"A real dustcloth?"

"Who is the manager here, you or I?" retorts Granovsky.

My poor heart!

Papa, Mama!

Naturally, in my opinion, the first performance did not have perfect unity.

But I felt that my task was finished.

And then the Habima theatre asked me to take in hand the settings for "The Dibbuk."

I didn't know what to do.

At that time the two theatres were at war.

But I could not refuse to go to that "Habima" where the actors did not act but prayed, they too, alas, lauding to the skies the dramatic art of Stanislavsky.

If our romance with Granovsky "didn't take" as he put it, I was even farther from Wachtangoff. Manager of Habima, as well as actor in the Stanislavsky theatre, his productions were, at that period, still unknown.

It was hard for me to establish a common basis of communication with him.

I respond to love, but confronted with doubts, hesitations, I draw back.

When I attended the first performances of "The Dibbuk" and listened to Wachtangoff, I thought:

He is a Georgian.

This is the first time we have met. He is silent. We examine each other awkwardly. Surely he can read in my eyes the chaos and unrest of the East, a strange, incomprehensible art.

But what is the use of worrying, blushing and glaring

at him? I'm going to inject a drop of poison into him.

With me, or behind my back, he will remember it one day. Others will come after me and will translate my words and my sighs into a more popular, lighter and clearer form.

At last Zemach, the manager of Habima, rouses me from my thoughts.

"Marc Zacharovitch, in your opinion, how should 'The Dibbuk' be staged?"

"You'd better consult Wachtangoff first," I replied.

A pause.

Wachtangoff says, slowly, that all these deformations are foreign to him, that the Stanislavsky method is the right one.

Seldom have I been so beside myself with rage.

"In that case why did you bother me?"

But, controlling myself, I answer that I cannot see that method in the renaissance of the Jewish theatre.

And, turning to Zemach:

"Nevertheless, you will stage it my way, even if I am not there; there is no other way."

And having got that off my chest, I walked out.

On the way home I recalled my first meeting with Ansky, the author of "The Dibbuk."

He caught sight of me at a reception, came over and embraced me and told me joyfully:

"You know, I have a play, 'The Dibbuk.' You are the only one who can bring it out. I've thought of you."

The writer, Baal-Machschowess, who was with us, smiled and nodded and even his glasses bobbed in agreement.

But what can I do?

Some time afterwards I was told that, one year later, Wachtangoff spent hours before my murals in Granovsky's theatre, and at Habima (Zemach admitted it to me himself), they ordered another artist to paint "à la Chagall."

I also heard that, at Granovsky's, they were now going beyond Chagall!

Good for them!

While working in the theatre I did not forget that my family was living in Malachowka, in a little country village near Moscow.

To reach it, I first had to queue up for several hours to buy my ticket, then another hour to get as far as the station platform.

Dressed in my smock and wide trousers I had difficulty in withstanding the pressure of the crowd.

Throngs of milkmaids banged their white tin cans mercilessly into my back. They trampled on my feet. Peasants pushed and shoved.

Standing or stretched out on the ground they busily hunted lice.

Sunflower seeds cracked between their teeth and spurted out on my hands, on my face.

At last when towards nightfall the icy train slowly got under way, songs, plaintive and boisterous, resounded in the smoke-filled car.

It seemed to me I was going up to heaven through birchwoods, snow and clouds of smoke, with all those plump women, those bearded peasants tirelessly making their signs of the Cross.

A number of cans, empty of milk, but filled with coins, rattled like drums.

At last the train stops and I get out. So it goes day after day.

It is night: I cross deserted fields and I think I see a wolf crouched in the snow.

A wolf—no doubt about it.

I turn aside, step back, then move forward cautiously until I'm sure it isn't a wolf. Only a poor dog lying there, motionless.

In the morning I take the same road back to Moscow.

It is not yet day. The sky is lilac blue. The plain envelops you with its thousands of miles. Joyous birches crown your head.

On the platform again, troops of milkmaids with their cans of milky water: the same peasants stinking to high heaven.

The freight train lumbers along, crackling with cold.

People hurry, jostling one another as they rush for the icy steps.

Suddenly, a sharp cry. A peasant woman has fallen flat in the snow under the wheels of a car; she shrieks wildly.

Violet blood from her broken leg spreads over the snow.

"Oh! my brothers!" we can hear her moaning.

They dig, they shovel, they lift her and carry her off like so much manure.

Now we've seen all sorts of things.

20

The Narkompross invites me to come as a professor to the children's colony known as the "Third International," and also to the colony at Malachowka.

These colonies are composed of some fifty children each, all orphans, under the supervision of intelligent teachers who dreamed of applying the most advanced pedagogic methods.

Those children had been the most unhappy of orphans.

All of them had been thrown out on the street, beaten by thugs, terrified by the flash of the dagger that cut their parents' throats. Deafened by the whistling of bullets and the crash of broken windowpanes, they still heard, ringing in their ears, the dying prayers of their fathers and mothers. They had seen their father's beard savagely torn out, their sisters raped, disemboweled.

Ragged, shivering with cold and hunger, they roamed the cities, clung on to the bumpers of trains until, at last —a few thousand among so many, many others—they were taken into shelters for children.

And here they are before me.

They live in several different country houses, but come together only for their lessons.

In winter their little houses are buried in snow, and the wind, raising whirls of snowflakes, whistles and sings in the chimneys.

The children busy themselves with housework, taking turns preparing their meals, baking their bread, cutting and hauling their firewood, washing and mending.

Like grown men they hold meetings, deliberate and pass judgment on one another. They even judge their teachers and sing in chorus the International, waving their arms and smiling.

I taught those unfortunate little ones art.

Barefoot, lightly clad, each one shouted louder than the other: "Comrade Chagall, Comrade Chagall!" . . . The clamor came from every side.

Only their eyes would not, or could not, smile.

I loved them. They drew pictures. They flung themselves at colors like wild beasts at meat.

One of the boys seemed to be in a perpetual frenzy of creation. He painted, composed music and wrote verses.

Another boy constructed his art calmly, like an engineer.

Certain of them, devoted themselves to abstract art, approaching in this way the work of Cimabue and the art of stained-glass windows.

I was entranced by their drawings, their inspired stammerings and this lasted until the moment when I was obliged to give them up.

What has become of you, my dear little ones?

When I think of you, my heart bleeds.

To be closer to the colony at Malachowka, I had been assigned an unfurnished little wooden villa. However, it had a garret where we could live.

Our single iron bed was so narrow that, by morning, your body was sore and bruised.

But, managing to find some trestles, we were able by this means to enlarge our bed somewhat.

That house still held the odor of its refugee owners, the suffocating odor of contagious diseases. On every side lay medicine bottles, filth left by domestic animals.

Summer and winter the windows stayed wide open.

Below, in the communal kitchen, a hilarious peasant woman presided over our meals.

Laughing and showing all her teeth, as she put the bread in the oven, she talked frankly about her adventures.

"During the famine," she said, "I managed with difficulty to get some bags of flour in country towns some distance from here. I brought them home on freight trains.

"Once, in the train," she went on, laughing, "I ran into a patrol of twenty-five militiamen. I was alone in the car.

"It's against the law to bring in flour," they said. "Don't you know that?"

"Eh! Well! So I lay down. All twenty-five of them came, one by one. And I stayed there on that bench.

"In exchange they let me bring back my bag of flour."

I looked her straight in the face.

That night, she went down to the ground floor where the forest guards lodged.

After a while it was obvious that she was pregnant. And she stayed permanently with the forest guards.

If only they don't all come up to our place, armed with their hatchets!

I wait patiently in the anteroom of the Narkompross until the head of the office is pleased to receive me.

I want, if possible, to get them to set a price for the murals I painted for the theatre.

If not in "the first category"—the one that artists

more adept than I easily obtain—then at least let them give me the minimum rate.

The manager smiles.

"Yes . . . yes . . . you understand," he stammers, "the estimate . . . signatures, seals . . . Lunacharsky. Come back tomorrow."

That went on for two years.

I got . . . pneumonia. Granovsky smiled, too.

What else could I do?

My God! Granted, you have given me talent—at least so they say. But why didn't you give me an imposing face so that people would fear and respect me?

If, for example, I were large and fat, extremely tall, with long legs and a square head, then they would hold me in awe, the way it usually goes in this world.

But my face is too soft. My voice does not carry.

I am in despair.

I roam the streets of Moscow.

As I pass the Kremlin, I peer furtively through the vast gates.

Trotsky gets out of his car; he is tall, his nose bluish-red. With a bold, heavy tread he crosses the threshold and walks towards his apartment in the Kremlin.

An idea strikes me: what if I were to call on the poet, Demyan Bedny, who also lives in the Kremlin and with whom, during the war, I served on the same military committee.

I'll enlist his aid and Lunacharsky's for permission to go back to Paris.

I've had enough of being a teacher, a director.

I want to paint my pictures.

173   All my prewar canvases are in Berlin and in Paris where my studio, filled with sketches and unfinished pictures, is waiting for me.

From Germany, my good friend the poet Rubiner wrote me:

"Are you alive? There is a rumor you have been killed in the war.

"Do you realize you are famous here? Your pictures have introduced a new genre: expressionism. They're selling for high prices. Just the same, don't count on the money Walden owes you. He won't pay you, for he maintains that the glory is enough for you!"

Well, it can't be helped!

I would rather think about my relatives, Rembrandt, my mother, Cézanne, my grandfather, my wife.

I would have gone to Holland, to the south of Italy, to Provence, and stripping off my clothes I would have said:

"My dears, you see I've come back to you. I'm sad here. The only thing I want is to make pictures and something else.

Neither Imperial Russia, nor the Russia of the Soviets needs me.

They don't understand me. I am a stranger to them.

I'm certain Rembrandt loves me.

21

These pages have the same meaning as a painted surface.

If there were a hiding place in my pictures, I would slip them into it . . . Or perhaps they would cling to the back of one of my characters or maybe to the trousers of the "Musician" in my mural painting? . . .

Who can know what is written on his back?

In the era of the R.S.F.S.R. I shout at will:

Don't you feel our electric scaffoldings slip under our feet?

And were not the forewarnings in our plastic art right—since we are truly up in the air and suffer from one malady only—the hankering for stability.

Those five years churn in my soul.

I have grown thin. I'm even hungry.

I long to see you again, B . . . , C . . . , P . . . . I am tired.

I shall come with my wife, my child.

I shall lie down near you.

And, perhaps, Europe will love me and, with her, my Russia.

Moscow, 1922.

note on this edition

Marc Chagall wrote his autobiography in Russian during his stay in Moscow in 1921-22. He was then thirty-five years old. Paul Cassirer, a Berlin publisher, planned to publish the autobiography together with a number of the author's etchings and dry points, but this volume never appeared. Instead, Cassirer simply published a portfolio of twenty etchings and dry points, under the title *Mein Leben*. Chagall's autobiography was not published until 1932, in the French translation by his wife Bella. This volume, *Ma Vie,* was published by Librairie Stock.

This first American edition, which includes the twenty illustrations first published by Paul Cassirer, has been translated from the 1957 reprint of the Bella Chagall translation.

glossary

Badchan: a street singer or minstrel who officiates at weddings as singer and master of ceremonies.

Cheder (Hebrew, "Room"): Hebrew elementary school.

Goubispolkom: Russian abbreviation for Soviet Government.

Haggadah (Hebrew, "Story, narrative"): the part of the Talmud which is the aesthetic and literary element of the Oral Law (allegories, parables, legends, tales).

Kadet: from 1904 to 1917 the party of the Constitutional Democrats (K.D.) in Russia.

Kasha: Buckwheat, semolina or groats cooked with red fruit juices.

Narkom: Russian abbreviation for People's Commissar.

Narkompross: Russian abbreviation for the Ministry of Education in the Soviet Republic.

R.S.F.S.R.: Russian Socialist Federation of Soviet Republics.

Simhath Torah: Festival of the Rejoicing of the Law.

Sovnarkom: Russian abbreviation for Council of People's Commissars.

Sukkoth: Feast of Tabernacles.

Synhedrion: the higher courts of law.

Talis: a prayer robe.

Tefillin: phylacteries, scrolls inscribed with biblical texts that are worn on the arm and head during the daily morning worship.

Vasistas: fanlight, or transom.